Former bartender, bar director, and celebrated industry leader John deBary takes a back-to-basics, nonjudgmental, and distinctly playful approach to the science of making great cocktails at home. With a mix of humor and realness, he helps you understand the elements that make a drink objectively good, like the perfect serving temperature and the just-right balance of sweet, acid, and bitter. Then, with that foundational knowledge, John gives you permission to tweak and tinker cocktails to best suit your taste buds, mood, available ingredients, and pretty much any set of circumstances.

Stuck at your in-laws'? There's a flowchart to guide you from a neglected liquor cabinet to a tasty drink. **Need a buzz by the ocean?** Freeze a Beached Mint-Lime Cooler overnight and let it defrost to deliciousness on your way. **Want to surprise yourself and your friends?** Try an umami-forward Soy Sauce Old Fashioned. John even has an entire chapter for making nonalcoholic cocktails that are just as sophisticated as those with spirits. Along with recipes, he includes exercises to help you practice your flavor-balancing skills, as well as *all* the details on liquors, mixers, shaking, stirring, and much more. Overflowing with John's 100-proof personality, *Drink What You Want* will have you laughing just as much as you are experimenting with mixology. This book will empower you to craft drinks to your preference—and to find the drinks you love.

Drink What You Want

The **Subjective** Guide to Making **Objectively** Delicious Cocktails

John deBary

Illustrations by Sarah Tanat-Jones

Clarkson Potter/Publishers
New York

Published in the United States by Clarkson Potter/
Publishers, an imprint of Random House, a division of
Penguin Random House LLC, New York.
clarksonpotter.com

CLARKSON POTTER is a trademark and POTTER with
colophon is a registered trademark of Penguin
Random House LLC.

Library of Congress Cataloging-in-Publication Data
Names: DeBary, John, author.
Title: Drink what you want : the subjective guide to
making objectively delicious cocktails / John DeBary ;
illustrations by Sarah Tanat-Jones
Description: First Edition. | New York : Clarkson Potter,
2020. | Includes index. |
Identifiers: LCCN 2019037791 (print) | LCCN
2019037792 (ebook) | ISBN 9780525575771
(hardcover) | ISBN 9780525575788 (ebook)
Subjects: LCSH: Cocktails. | Alcoholic beverages. |
LCGFT: Cookbooks
Classification: LCC TX951 .D387 2020 (print) | LCC
TX951 (ebook) | DDC 641.87/4—dc23
LC record available at https://lccn.loc.gov/2019037791
LC ebook record available at https://lccn.loc.
gov/2019037792

ISBN 978-0-525-57577-1
Ebook ISBN 978-0-525-57578-8

Printed in China

Book design by Ian Dingman
Illustrations by Sarah Tanat-Jones

10 9 8 7 6 5 4 3 2 1

First Edition

To my husband, Michael, who puts up with A LOT

Contents

FOREWORD

I faced unusual circumstances in the months leading up to the opening of PDT in May 2007: there were very few bartenders in New York City interested in preparing what we now call craft cocktails. The mere mention of a mojito elicited deep eye rolls among my peers, so instead of pandering for their participation, I hired a handful of the willing from Manhattan's seven other serious cocktail lounges and supplemented the staff with a cadre of amateur enthusiasts.

My approach to this dilemma—hiring for enthusiasm versus experience—marked the end of my embrace of the hiring hierarchy I came up in, which was modeled on a caste-like seniority structure in the front and back of the house. The decision was enabled, ironically, by a burgeoning financial crisis—buttressed by mounting student debts—that led a generation of young adults from supportive families and college into the food and beverage industry instead of the cubicles of corporate America. PDT was a direct beneficiary.

For the first time in my career, I was surrounded by a team with the emotional and intellectual faculties to diligently question everything I showed them, which forced me to put my own learnings to the test every day I turned up on St. Mark's Place. John deBary, who joined us a year after we opened, was one of these colleagues whose rigorous, open-minded methodology is outlined in this choose-your-own-adventure-style cocktail book.

A Columbia grad (we had five, beginning with Don Lee, who staffed the bar like it was an alumni association), John was raised in Greenwich, Connecticut, by a Wall Street lawyer who just so happened to pen his own drinks primer, *The Persistent Observer's Guide to Wine*. In his introduction to this book, John claims he was anxious to pass my muster when Don hired him, but I'd argue it was I who was on the back of my heels with deBary, whose father's book title cannily characterizes his son.

John stuck around for five years. He created cocktails like the Shark, Kansai Kick, and Mill Valley Cooler (all chronicled here) that had long, profitable runs on the bar menu. He accompanied me on trips to Tokyo (he speaks and writes Japanese) and Paris, where we "popped up" to bring our New York City speakeasy experience overseas. He was behind the bar when we were recognized at the top of the prestigious World's 50 Best Bars list in 2011 and the following year, when we received the first-ever James Beard Outstanding Bar Program award.

When we weren't tending bar together, we collaborated on *Food & Wine*'s annual cocktail book, which John edited as my deputy under Kate Krader for two years (2012 and 2013) and then on his own for another two with Kate (2015 and 2016). In 2009, he began splitting time between PDT and Momofuku, until he left outright in 2013 to open a total of ten restaurants in David Chang's dynasty. As I look back, this "persistent observer" went from blazing a trail alongside me to blowing past me in new directions.

It came as little surprise when John signed a book deal and founded his own drinks company: I had done these things, too. What piqued my interest (okay, it shocked me) was the frankness with which he began expressing himself on social media after he moved on from PDT. This matter-of-fact point of view continues here in what serves as the cocktail book equivalent of *Go the F*ck to Sleep* to an audience (me) more accustomed to books (mine) that read like *Goodnight Moon*.

Indeed, there are passages here that would cause the Marquis de Sade to blush: I won't spoil them for you. As I both cackled out loud and winced from page to page—wondering if I was really the best person to recommend this book—it eventually dawned on me that John's book is the coming-out party the genre desperately needs.

Bars and the patrons who frequent them are colorful, cultured, profound, and profane, like deBary himself. In numerous artfully placed footnotes, John reveals the logic behind his mixological musings like David Foster Wallace in drag. The blistering sarcasm of his self-conscious asides stands shoulders above humorless heterosexual cis drinks writers of today (hello!), whose bland perspective reflects neither the diversity nor the dynamism of America's barrooms and bartenders.

John's cocky, idiosyncratic, culturally literate, OCD voice is like the subject matter itself: bold, brash, bitter, exacting, and occasionally scandalous. His book is the Corpse Reviver (Number Blue, of course) bartenders and enthusiasts have been thirsting for. For this, and to witness John step out as he does ahead, I'm honored to position the coaster.

—Jim Meehan, founder of PDT, author, and owner of Mixography, Inc.

INTRODUCTION

About Me

Enough about you—let's start with me. I've been working as a bar professional for about ten years and I've been fortunate enough to have spent time behind the bar at some of the best spots in the world. But, like many in my industry, my path into the bar world was anything but straightforward.

I grew up in a fancy suburb of New York City, went to a fancy college in Manhattan, and until I ended up behind the bar, I was on track to become a lawyer or academic or something similarly white-collar. I had a vague idea that I needed a "real" job to be successful in life and I never imagined bartending would be the way I would do it.

I studied Japanese history and language in college and moved to Japan after graduation. I was considering staying there indefinitely, but after about three months, I realized it wasn't the place for me and returned to New York City. With no job and a few grand in credit card debt, I was fairly desperate and asked everyone I'd ever known if they could hook me up with a job— any job. One of those people was Don Lee, a guy I went to college with who was on the opening team of the iconic reservations-only cocktail bar PDT (Please Don't Tell) on St. Mark's Place in the East Village. This was a year or two before it became the legendary spot it is today. I asked Don if I could come bartend there and, astonishingly, he agreed to let me train. Mind you, I had no bar, spirits, or cocktail experience whatsoever. But after a couple of shifts, I started to get the hang of it. And by the hang of it, I mean flat-out pretending that I knew what the fuck I was doing. I was the queen of "fake it 'til you make it."

With three or four more shifts under my belt, I was feeling pretty good about this new gig, but I still had to pass the Jim Meehan test. In case you don't know, Jim was the Big Boss of PDT at the time and he was a big deal well before the bar was. I was so nervous to meet him; I thought he would see right through me for the fraud that I was. Fortunately, he didn't, and I was permitted to keep showing up at PDT every Monday night even though I was Some Dude with No Experience Who Still Wanted to Go to Law School.

I was twenty-five years old, which is kind of old relative to when a lot of people start out in the food service industry, and I knew I needed to catch up fast. So I hit the books: Gary Regan's *The Joy of Mixology*, David Wondrich's *Imbibe!*, and David Embury's *The Fine Art of Mixing Drinks* were the first of the hundreds of cocktail books I would read. I understood that I needed to stop pretending I knew what a Sazerac was and actually learn how to make one—and also learn there was a whiskey called Sazerac as well—so I devoured the Rolodex* of cocktail recipes that sat behind the bar at PDT by transcribing them into my personal notebook and making flash cards to study.

Eventually, instead of feeling profound panic at the beginning of my shift,† I eased into a sense of comfort. After a few quick months, my name and picture were featured in *The New York Times* as one of the geeky bartenders at this cool new underground cocktail bar. The article helped me realize I was onto something with the cocktail thing. My law school dreams evaporated.

A year after starting my career at PDT, I was offered a job bartending twice a week at Momofuku Ssäm Bar, the second restaurant to open in the now-global empire of chef David Chang. In case you haven't watched TV or looked at the internet or a newspaper in the past fifteen years, David Chang is a chef from Virginia who rose to culinary prominence with the opening of Momofuku Noodle Bar in 2007. Now the group has a dozen restaurants spanning the globe and has spawned magazines, cookbooks, sauces, podcasts, and more Netflix specials than I have the inclination to count (or time to actually watch).

Apart from teaching me about wine, service, kitchen techniques, and how

---

* Literally, we had three Rolodexes full of cocktail recipes. This was before smartphones, kids.
† I didn't yet know I had OCD and an anxiety disorder.

to disarm grumpy chefs, my time there gave me my first opportunity to exercise creativity over an entire cocktail menu, not just individual drinks. After about three years behind the bar, I transitioned to becoming the company's first bar director, a position I held for five years. During that time, I helped open more than ten restaurants, created dozens of cocktail menus, and trained countless people on how to bartend.

And now I get to teach you how to make great drinks.

About You

Ultimately this book is for everyone. But if you've never made a drink in your entire life and don't know the difference between an Old Fashioned and a gin and tonic, you are my target demographic. My goal is to bring you to a point of reasonable proficiency and comfort in drink-making without getting too bogged down in the nerdy details that can scare many away.

If you like making drinks, own a few cocktail books, have figured out your favorite Scotch, and want to get a little more creative while making your life easier and more delicious, this book is also for you, but you might see some familiar things.

If you're a seasoned professional with years of experience behind the bar and you've read all the classics, regularly develop drink recipes, design bars and menus, and train people to become bartenders, I hope you'll find this book is also for you. You'll probably encounter facts and recipes that are totally familiar, but hopefully, hearing these things from a fresh perspective—mine—can help you organize your thoughts and in turn be better at what you do. You might hate me for some of the things I'll say. Hell, I hate me for some of the things I say. You also might consider my advice heretical, sloppy, and full of gross overgeneralizations. I don't deny any of those things. But I invite you to consider the viewpoint that compromise and simplification are sometimes necessary in many situations. Although carelessness is never okay. Look, if you think I've got something really wrong and you want to yell at me about it, please do. I've been wrong many times in the past and I'm sure I will be wrong many times in the future. I'm @jnd3001 on Twitter and Instagram, and I love it when people talk shit about me on the internet, mostly because I love attention.

No matter who you are or how much you know about spirits, bartending, and cocktails, I'm going to write as though you, dear reader, know absolutely nothing. Don't be offended. Feel free to skip ahead or jump around, but just know that sometimes the best way to learn is to relearn with a beginner's mind-set.

Regardless of all of the above, thank you for buying* this book, and please keep reading.

About This Book

I want you to use this book to learn how to make great cocktails. In order to make great cocktails, you must first understand what a cocktail is. Don't worry, I'll walk you through that, and you'll learn what goes into making cocktails objectively—and subjectively—delicious. Then we get to the drinks. I've organized the chapters according to mood, feeling, situation— basically according to how these drinks make me feel, or according to what I want to drink when I feel a certain way. These are the cocktails I believe are truly great.

A few caveats before you get started: Making cocktails at home isn't easy, even for someone with tons of experience. When removed from the cocktail

---

* Or stealing; I don't know your life.

bar or restaurant setting, there's more preparation required. Remember, at bars and restaurants, there are literally teams of people who work for hours just to set up a bar, keep it stocked, and scrub it clean at the end of the night. Most people aren't prepared for how messy at-home cocktailing is— your floor will be sticky, your cabinets will be sticky, and, yeah, your ceiling will probably also be sticky. You will use a soul-crushing amount of ice. You will probably run out of citrus faster than you would ever expect, and you will most likely get a lot drunker than you planned.*

But here's what I want you to take away: While there are certain rules for making great drinks, not everything is for everybody, and chances are you won't like 100% of the drinks in this book. I can live with that, and you should be able to, too. Yes, there are some structural elements that make drinks objectively good or bad—and we'll get to that—but ultimately, everyone is different. The importance of your own experience and opinions and taste cannot and should not be understated. There is good pop music and bad pop music, but if you just don't like pop, no amount of listening to Kylie Minogue songs—some of the best pop music in history—will make you like her. You're not a bad person! You just know what you like.† Same goes for cocktails. If you're a garbage person and like garbage drinks, great; if you think you're fancy and are fastidious about what graces your palate, I might find you intolerable as a human, but you have every right to live your life the way you want and to drink what you want.

After reading this book, I want you to have the knowledge, skills, and confidence to make drinks on your own. I want to teach you that there are a small number of archetypal drink recipes whose patterns are endlessly riffed to create new drinks; how to master ingredients, tools, and techniques; and how to use this knowledge to confidently make great drinks under any circumstances.

---

* Okay, maybe that's just me?

† But I urge you to watch the video for "Get Outta My Way" before coming to any definitive conclusions about Kween Kylie.

BACKGROUND INFORMATION

What Is a Cocktail?

It sounds like a dumb question, but I'd wager that only a few people can answer it definitively. Some may have an intuitive sense of the definition, but I would venture that when pressed to actually define the word "cocktail," to denote where the lines are drawn around it, both philosophically and technically, they'd come up with nothing—or nothing helpful, at least. I can't help but be reminded of the famous 1964 US Supreme Court quotation regarding the definition of obscenity: "I know it when I see it." I imagine that a lot of people have the same approach here.

Why is it helpful—or even interesting—for us to define the word "cocktail"? Well, if we develop a more inclusive and expansive definition of what a cocktail is, we can be more comfortable and confident when making one. A more inclusive definition is important because it will help you to see that you're probably already making cocktails for yourself—you just don't realize it—and that it's way easier than you might think.

Here is my definition: A cocktail is a drink made by mixing two or more things together.

That's it. That's the definition.

If you put a specific amount of cream and sugar in your coffee, you're literally making a cocktail. Congratulations.

Deliciousness: Objective vs. Subjective

I have thought a lot about why some things taste good and others do not, and it's hard to pin down the exact source of deliciousness in the world. Is there innate deliciousness in foods? Or is it all in our heads?* The answer is, as you might imagine, quite complex. Yes, there are substances in the world that humans inherently find delicious—things that contain sugar, protein, and fat—because we need nutrients in order to survive, so we have a built-in tendency to want to consume things that contain them. That's the objective, data-driven, fact-based truth. But deliciousness is not that simple. Our opinions, memories, associations, tastes—the subjective—add a layer on top of that. That's deliciousness.

It's when you satisfy both that you have a great drink.† A truly great cocktail is both objectively and subjectively delicious.

Objective deliciousness is analytical: How sweet is it? Is it too strong? Too bitter? When it comes to cocktails, objective deliciousness can easily be broken down and quantified. There are rules and regulations that have generally been accepted, practiced, and taught. And we'll get to that in just a moment.

But subjective deliciousness is emotional: Do you *like* the drink? Does it make sense, given your mood? Do you like how it makes you feel? You can make the most perfectly crafted eggnog (see page 165) in the world, but if you drink it while you're on a hot, sweaty beach, you're probably going to have a

---

* Like everything?
† Or a great anything. But for our purposes, a great drink.

bad time. I have served two people the exact same cocktail within the span of ten minutes and one of them has said it's the best of their life and the other has sent it back.

Simply put, subjective deliciousness is people's preferences—their likes and dislikes. We can't package it into neat categories the way we can objective deliciousness.* Not only are our preferences all unique, but they can also vary considerably in the same person under different circumstances. How many times have you been running around on a hot day and ice water was literally the most delicious thing you've ever tasted in your entire life? Probably not so in the middle of a sloshy, freezing hailstorm when you forgot to wear that jacket with a hood. And how many times have you scarfed down an entire bag of gummi bears where the first few are a tasty delight, but you eat the last half of the bag only out of a sense of obligation and, well, you're already crying, so why stop now? Depending on how you feel, a given drink can be either a lifesaver or a vile poison.

You can also like and dislike a drink based on an emotional reaction to a memory: "I love absinthe because it reminds me of my summer in Paris," or "My asshole ex-boyfriend drank Scotch all the time and now I can't smell it without gagging."

People who say they only think "rationally" or "logically" about cocktails (or anything, really) are lying. Emotion, feeling, mood, situation, whatever you want to call it, provides the context for our entire experience of the world—and it is the most important element of deliciousness. Everyone is different, and even when a drink is made well, it fails when the person drinking it simply doesn't like it. When it comes to subjective versus objective, subjective will always win.

Now, I can't help you understand your emotions, no matter how many drunk DMs you send me. That's a layer you're going to have to interpret on your own time, for yourself—or at least with a therapist. But I can help you understand what makes a cocktail objectively good. If you want to gain a better understanding of where your subjective balance preferences interplay with the objective, Appendix A (page 211) details a few exercises you can conduct to help you explore exactly that and hopefully give you a more intuitive sense of what makes a cocktail taste good—to you.

---

* And even when dealing with objective deliciousness, each person is unique because genetics plays a huge role in how our senses function. But let's not get into that in this book, k?

The Elements of a Balanced Cocktail

We use our mouths and taste buds to determine objective deliciousness in six distinct ways. Drinks can be balanced and delicious without hitting each balance point discussed here, but these dimensions of objective deliciousness are the most significant in assessing the success or failure of a given cocktail.

1. ALCOHOL

Alcohol tastes hot and spicy to us. Balanced drinks blend this sensation harmoniously with their other ingredients. Essentially, if a drink is too strong or too weak, that means its alcohol is out of balance.* The sensation of alcohol should be perceptible but not overpowering. Additionally, alcohol acts on our brain and nervous system to make us feel different. One of the most important—but often overlooked—elements of serving great drinks is the art of not accidentally serving people too much alcohol.

2. SWEETNESS

Sweetness is the sensation that lets us know something contains sugar. Sweetness is the taste sense that people have explored the most in their lives; it's the taste that develops first when we're babies, and our desire for it tends to diminish as we age. Many people say they like drinks with low

---

* Obviously cocktails that do not contain alcohol need not concern themselves with this.

sweetness, but if you were to actually give them a bone-dry drink without any, they would find it undrinkable. Basically, people overstate their aversion to sweetness, most likely due to a past experience with an imbalanced, overly sweet cocktail and a desire to appear sophisticated.

Cocktails must contain a certain degree of sweetness, even if they do not taste noticeably sweet. Sweetness primarily balances out the spirits and acidity in a cocktail, and it provides body—an important feature of a good cocktail. So what's body, you ask? You know how some drinks have a great mouth-filling texture* and a long and satisfying finish? That is body, and it is the result of the presence of some sugar in the drink. Sugar is literally sticky, so the drink sticks (sorry) around longer in your mouth and throat after you swallow. Most people find the persistence of a cocktail's flavors enjoyable. So don't be afraid of sugar.

3. ACIDITY

Acidity is the counterpoint to sweetness. Most people use words like *tart* and *sour* to describe the sensation of that saliva-inducing pinch in the corners of your mouth when you're drinking something with tons of acidity. Sometimes people mistakenly

refer to this as "bitterness," which is a completely different sensation (we're getting to it, hold on). Acidity is important because it imparts a bright vibrancy to cocktails, making them uplifting and refreshing, and acid is extremely helpful in balancing out sweetness.

Some people are total acid junkies (me) and love a drink with screaming acidity—almost purposefully out of balance—but most normal people are happy when a cocktail contains an equal volume of something sweet and something acidic so that neither sensation is too prominent.

Not every drink contains acidity, however. Drinks like Old Fashioneds (page 71) and Manhattans (page 75) don't really have any significant acidity for us to worry about, and that's okay.

4. BITTERNESS

Bitterness is scary to us as humans, because it signals poison. As babies, we are pre-programmed not to want to eat poison. This is why bitterness is considered an acquired taste—we have to learn, through experience, that bitter drinks will (probably) not kill us, and that the bitterness is actually enjoyable in measured doses. I compare bitterness to roller coasters: The first time I went on one, I thought I was going to die,

---

* Don't say *mouthfeel*, please.

but after a few rides, I was loving it. I learned that the experience was safe, and that safe danger is thrilling. Most people need to try coffee or spicy foods a few times before they learn to love them, and the same goes for bitter drinks.

Bitterness is a fascinating sense because, unlike sweet and sour, for which our taste buds have one type of receptor (the cell that transmits information about the environment to our nervous system and brain), we detect bitterness with about twenty-five different types of receptors, meaning that we can detect many distinct variations of bitterness.

Bitter drinks also have a functional benefit, especially around mealtime. The perception of bitterness activates systems in our body that respond to poisoning, namely our digestion and elimination systems. A light, bitter drink such as an Old Pal (page 115) before a meal can help stimulate the appetite, and afterward, something a little more intense, like a Vieux Carré (page 118), can help us feel settled after indulging.

Drinks can be bitter subtly or overtly. Use a dash or two of cocktail bitters such as Angostura to season your cocktails—just enough so that there's a nice bite to the drink. Cocktails that have larger volumes of bitter ingredients, like amaro or aromatized wine, are balanced when their bitterness is perceptible, but

not to the point where it overrides the rest of the elements.

5. TEMPERATURE

Temperature plays a huge role in our enjoyment of cocktails. Generally, and with few exceptions, we like cocktails—and most drinks, for that matter—cold. Cold temperatures decrease the perception of alcohol and sweetness, allowing the sugar to do its job: provide body and finish without being cloying. Cold temperatures reduce the volatility of aromatics, meaning that the perception of aromas and flavors is reduced. This can help in cocktails with lots of strongly flavored components. You don't want to freeze anyone's tongue, but you do need to make sure your cocktail is properly chilled in order for it to be objectively delicious.*

6. DILUTION

In most cocktails, dilution comes from water that's melted off the ice you use to chill the drink—the room-temperature ingredients transfer their warmth to the ice, and the ice melts.

Dilution is important because spirits can contain a tremendous amount of flavor, and mixing them with a bit of

---

* Yes, yes, I know that there are many valid room-temperature and hot cocktail recipes out there. But we only discuss cold drinks in this book, with one or two outlier exceptions. I don't even follow my own rules.

water lowers the overall concentrations of flavor-containing molecules, allowing us to perceive more subtlety. Straight out of the bottle, spirits are generally about 40% alcohol by volume (ABV), and diluting them closer to 20% ABV by mixing them with other ingredients makes them taste better. Lemon and lime juice—common ingredients in cocktails—also taste much better when their screaming acidity is slightly watered down.

In objectively delicious drinks, about one quarter of the volume consists of melted ice. The exception is a drink that has any kind of supplementary water added to it, such as a Tom Collins (page 91) or Highball (pageg 87). In those cases, the balance comes from slight over-dilution, because that's the goal of the drink.

What Does All This Mean?

In order to make truly great cocktails, we need to approach our drink-making from both the objective and subjective angles. From here on out, I will be giving you a lot of objective information, like how to find the best tequila or how to make ginger syrup. All of this information is meaningless if it's not applied properly given subjective conditions. Every recipe in this book is *my* subjective best version of the drink based on my objective knowledge. Ultimately I want you to determine *your* subjective best versions, using what you've learned here as a foundation.

WHAT YOU NEED TO MAKE COCKTAILS

Ingredients

SPIRITS

The most significant ingredient in cocktails is spirits. Tons of books out there go into the production, styles, and history of spirits, and I would encourage any budding enthusiast to check them out—but this is not that book. If you want to explore spirits more deeply, take a look at my reading list in Appendix B (page 217). Here, I want to give you a quick-yet-meaningful summary of each spirit so you can start working on your own drinks without getting bogged down in things like the sad colonial history of rum. I'm also not going to be talking about every base spirit in the universe; rather, this is my personal roundup of my most useful base spirits, complete with my own biases and blind spots, but it's everything you need to know to use this book successfully.

Whiskey

Whiskey is an extremely broad category encompassing spirits from all over the world, made according to very different styles and traditions. The key defining characteristic of all whiskies is that they are made from grain and are aged in oak barrels.

BOURBON is an American whiskey made from a combination of corn, rye, barley, and wheat. By law it must contain at least 51% corn. The recipe is rounded out with rye and malted barley. Sometimes a producer will replace the rye with wheat, resulting in what's called, wait for it, a wheated bourbon. Maker's Mark is a notable example of this style, which is softer and gentler than other bourbons—a major reason, I suspect, for its enduring popularity.

By law, all American whiskey must be aged in new, charred American oak barrels, and bourbon is no exception. This aging process plays a huge role in the ultimate flavor of this whiskey, imparting toasty, nutty, caramel aromas while softening some of the harshness of the unaged spirit.

Bourbons can express themselves in varying ways depending on recipe, age, and other factors, but they are generally sweet and spicy with notes of caramel, toffee, banana, grass, and coconut. Bourbon mixes nicely with other flavors and is quite versatile.

Some of my favorite bourbons for cocktails are Maker's Mark, Wild Turkey, and Four Roses.

RYE is another American whiskey, made, unsurprisingly, from rye grain. It can, however, contain corn and malted barley and other grains if the distiller so chooses, as long as it contains at least 51% rye. Like bourbon, rye must be aged in new, charred American oak barrels for at least two years before bottling and can run the gamut from very cheap and shitty to very delicious and expensive. But cheap does not always mean shitty, and expensive does not always mean good.

In contrast to bourbon, rye is a bit spicier and has a sharp, grassy, and green cluster of flavors. I tend to favor rye slightly over bourbon in cocktails because its sharpness is a bit more apparent when mixed with other things. Every application has its own unique needs. There are plenty of drinks

Spirits, like beer and wine, contain alcohol, and alcohol is a product of fermentation. Fermentation occurs when yeast eats sugar and poops out ethanol, carbon dioxide, and other alcohols (plus a host of other chemicals with and without flavor). However, yeast can ferment only so much before its own activity makes its environment unsuitable to sustain its life. The alcohol by volume (ABV) achieved through fermentation tops out at about 20%. Most spirits are 40% or higher. Distillers (spirits producers) selectively remove water and other molecules from a fermented liquid to bring the ABV up to the desired level. The key thing to remember is that what sets spirits apart from the rest of the alcohol-containing beverages is distillation. Beer, wine, sake, and hard cider are not distilled—only fermented—and therefore are not spirits.

where bourbon is the superior choice, but I personally would always go for a Manhattan (page 75) or Old Fashioned (page 71) made with rye. One of my all-time favorites, the Vieux Carré (page 118), is a spectacular combination of rye and French brandy.

My go-to rye is Rittenhouse. It has that classic bite and it's cheap—but not shitty. Wild Turkey makes a nice rye, too.

SCOTCH WHISKY.* I consider Scotch to be the grandparent of whiskies, and many Scotch producers are considered the gold standard in terms of artistry and technical expertise.

As with American whiskies, there are a few rules for what can and cannot be called Scotch. The most significant of them dictate that Scotch whisky must be made in Scotland from cereal grain— most commonly barley—yeast, and water, and it must be aged for at least three years in oak. Barley is a cereal grain containing only starch, which is long chains of sugar. These chains must be broken so that yeast can do its work. This happens through malting, which is what happens when you allow the barley to sprout just slightly, releasing enzymes that break down starches.

Obviously, you don't want thousands of little barley plants in your whisky, so you have to kill them somehow. To do this, producers use indirect heat, such as an oven, or in the case of certain Scotches, smoke from burning peat, a fossilized plant matter that's a common fuel source in Scotland. Peat smoke has deep, green-black-tinged notes of petrol, eucalyptus, brine, low tide, and mint. Some producers use tons of peated barley in their production, while others use none.

Scotch producers are free to use a wide variety of barrels to age their whiskies, and ex-bourbon barrels are quite common. (Since American whiskey producers cannot reuse their barrels, there is a huge supply of used barrels.) Scotch is generally aged for a longer time than American whiskey and is lighter in color—more golden hay than rich amber. Some Scotches have age statements on them, saying the minimum amount of time they've been in barrel, but many don't.

There are two broad categories of Scotch: blends and single malts. Blends can be made up of whiskies from different grains and distilleries, while single malts must be made from 100% barley and by a single distiller in a single season.

For cocktails, blends without age statements work the best. Whiskies

---

* People spend a lot of effort distinguishing between the words "whiskey" and "whisky." I think it's good to know that generally "whiskey" refers to American and Irish products, and "whisky" refers to Scotch, Canadian, and Japanese. In order to speak about the broad global category of barrel-aged cereal-derived spirits, many contort themselves into awkward stylings like "whisk(ey)," or "whiskey/whisky." I find this unnecessary, so I'll be using "whiskey" when speaking generally because that's the American spelling and I am using American English. I'll use "whisky" when referring to Scotch, Canadian, and Japanese whisky.

The sun will still hang in the sky if you get this wrong—even Maker's Mark spells it "whisky" on their label. If anybody tries to make you feel bad about confusing the two spellings, they're not worth your time.

such as Compass Box's Great King Street and Highland Park's Magnus are delicious and reliable yet cheap enough that you don't feel like you're wasting too-good Scotch on a Rob Roy. In the realm of single malts, go for Ardbeg or Laphroaig if you want something intensely peaty. Oban and Glenmorangie are mellower and more honeyed, and more expensive.

IRISH WHISKEY. Like Scotch, Irish whiskey is made from barley and aged in reused barrels. My primary tasting note from barley-based spirits is stewed apples, and Irish whiskey gives me a decent amount of that. You'll get some char, smoke, and spice from the barrels as well.

As a base spirit, Irish whiskey works nicely with other flavors and can even skew fruity and refreshing in certain applications. Jameson is the most ubiquitous Irish whiskey by far and works well in many drinks, but others such as Powers and Bushmills are great alternatives if you want to veer off the beaten path.

JAPANESE WHISKY. At the beginning of the twentieth century, the Japanese decided they wanted to mimic the great whisky distilleries of Scotland. Japan is good at taking techniques and ideas from other cultures, studying and reverse-engineering them, and ultimately selling the product back to the originator for twice the price and at four times the quality. Japanese whisky is one of the most compelling examples of this pattern.

Japanese whisky is now regarded as some of the best and most sought-after in the world. It's slightly smoky, herbal, and totally unique. It has that mild apple flavor that I find common to barley-based whiskies.

Entry-level whiskies, such as Suntory's Toki and Hibiki Japanese Harmony, are excellent for use in cocktails. Mars is another great producer with a slightly richer style, and Nikka's whiskies are intense and robust but hard to find.

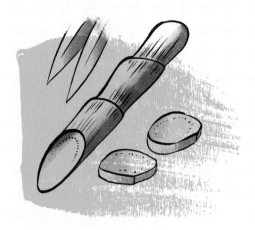

Rum

Rum is a tricky category to generalize about because it is so broad. Rum can be made anywhere and in a wide variety of styles, just as long as it is made from sugar. Most is made specifically from molasses. Some rum is aged in barrels, others not, and others still are aged and then filtered with charcoal to make them clear again.

Some rums can be complex, dark, and high-proof, while others can have near-vodka-like neutrality. However, I find there is a buttery note that seems to cut across the category. Sometimes grassy and banana-y flavors make their way in. There's usually an undercurrent of what I can only describe as "funk" somewhere in a rum, subtle as it may be.

Rum frequently gets pigeonholed into tropical applications, but thanks to the diversity of the spirit, you can use it in more than daiquiris and mai tais. Barrel-aged rums especially cross over into many applications where you might first think to use whiskey.

One of my go-to white rums is Flor de Caña four-year, which is an example of a rum that's been aged in ex-bourbon barrels and then filtered back to clarity. A unique-tasting rum from New York City is Owney's, and it has a delightful backstory that involves a disillusioned hedge fund manager, Far Rockaway speakeasies, and Irish rumrunners. (Google it.) For rum with more oak presence, I like Mount Gay XO and Banks 7 Golden Age.

Tequila

Tequila is made in the Mexican state of Jalisco from the agave plant. All spirits producers have a great deal of control over their finished product, but since many tequila producers grow their own agave, they have an added layer of control over their raw ingredients. Tequila is similar to wine in that the growing conditions play a large role in

the finished product. (Compare this to whiskey, where grain is grain no matter what the weather was like when it was growing.)

There are three main varieties of tequila: blanco, reposado, and añejo. Blanco tequila is unaged, and is sometimes referred to as "silver" because it's actually pretty sparkly when you look at it. Reposado tequilas are aged anywhere from three months to one year, and añejo tequilas are aged for at least one year and up to three. Producers can use a wide variety of barrels to age their tequilas, ranging from new oak to former wine casks.

For the most part, all tequilas taste in some degree like cooked agave, which, um, is what they're made from. This flavor is somewhere between pumpkin pie and maple syrup. Blanco tequilas tend to be bright, vegetal, sometimes floral or fruity, and some are a little olive-briney. Reposado and añejo tequilas contain those flavors as well, but by virtue of the aging process, they pick up the barrel's wood notes, such as caramel, vanilla, clove, and cinnamon. Añejos have these characteristics in greater intensity because they spend the most time in contact with the wood.

For me, blanco tequilas—along with gin and rye—are some of the most accessible base spirits to mix with. I find them chameleon-like, shape-shifting to whatever they're mixed with. They are the Odo of the spirits world.[*] They can

---

[*]   Shout-out to the four people who get this reference.

skew fruity and tropical, or they can go green and savory. The same is true for reposados and añejos; you just have to factor in the presence of oak. The more oak you get, the more you can treat the spirit as you would a whiskey. A Manhattan made with añejo tequila is a go-to riff of mine.

The thing about tequila is that if you want the good stuff, you're going to have to pay for it. You can buy cheap tequila, but it will likely be a *mixto*—an undrinkable version of tequila that's made with half agave, half whatever else is lying around, such as cheap neutral grain spirit. This is the type of tequila that many people first encounter, and it sets them up to think that all tequila is shitty because it tastes heinous and will give you a heinous hangover. When sourcing tequila, make sure it says "100% de Agave" on the label. The base price for good tequila is high but worth it. If you can find Cimarron Blanco, it's the best bet. Espolòn Blanco is decent and widely available. My all-time favorite, though, is Siete Leguas, whether for blanco, reposado, or añejo. El Tesoro's reposado is lovely as well.

Oh, also, mezcal. Mezcal is actually the broader category of agave-based spirits that tequila is a member of. There is so much to learn about mezcal: it is delicious and rustic, and its flavors can vary quite widely, more widely than tequila's. The gist of mezcal is that it has a somewhat similar flavor to blanco tequila but tends to be smoky due to the fact that the agave is cooked over an open flame—similar to how barley is cooked over peat smoke for Scotch. There are some exquisite and complex mezcals available, and those should generally be reserved for non-cocktail purposes. Two cocktail-suitable mezcals are Sombra and Vida.

Vodka

The name derives from the Russian word for "water," which is apt considering that vodka generally aspires to be as clean and neutral as possible—like water. Vodka can be distilled from any number of base ingredients: rye, corn, wheat, potatoes, and grapes, to name a few. Vodka must also be colorless and odorless, and to that end, many vodkas are filtered through charcoal.

Vodka gets a bad rap because it's kinda boring. I used to be that douche-bag bartender who talked shit about vodka and secretly* judged people who asked for vodka cocktails—sometimes I even tried to talk them out of their choice. But now I see that vodka is useful because it acts as a spacer, providing body and heat—from alcohol—while allowing the other flavors in whatever drink you're making to expand into the space that vodka creates.

Vodka is all about texture. The best vodkas are neutral and clean and have

---

* openly

a lush, smooth texture. Ketel One is made from wheat and has a lovely soft texture, so that's my go-to vodka. If I'm in the mood for something cheaper, Absolut—also made from wheat—is a great choice. For something a bit more original, Suntory's Haku vodka is made from rice and is very tasty.

Brandy

"Brandy" generally refers to a spirit made from distilled wine. I like to think of it as the umbrella term for anything made from fruit. But the two I talk about here are made from grapes specifically.

COGNAC/ARMAGNAC. I will probably piss off a lot of French people by lumping these two grape brandies together, but they are close enough for our purposes here. They are both made in France from white wine grapes and aged in oak barrels.

Cognac is generally a little softer and rounder, while Armagnac tends to be a bit more intense and rough around the edges. Treat Cognac as your default

brandy, and treat Armagnac more like a whiskey substitute and use it in place of rye or bourbon. A decent cocktail Cognac will set you back a little more than a gin, vodka, or American whiskey of similar quality because of its long aging in oak and the requirements of specific grape-growing areas. Pierre Ferrand Ambre is a go-to, as well as Paul Beau VS. You can find some bargains in Armagnac—I am partial to Marie Duffau's VSOP.

Pisco

Pisco is made in Peru from grapes. It does not see any oak aging and is distilled to a low proof. Most spirits are distilled to a very high concentration of alcohol and then diluted with pure water to bring it down to 40% ABV. Distillers do this in order to strip away the undesirable elements of a spirit, carving away exactly what they want before they add neutral-flavored water so people don't burn their mouths off. Not so with pisco. This means that a lot of the original characteristics of the wine make it into the bottle, giving it a full, lush texture.

I am partial to Macchu Pisco. It is made by two sisters, Melanie and Lizzie Asher, and has a vibrant, fresh acidity that's perfect for refreshing, happy drinks.

Gin

Gin is quite different from all the spirits we've discussed up to this point. Other spirits are made from a raw ingredient, the elements of which the producer retains in the finished product. Gin, alternatively, can almost be thought of as a flavored vodka. A gin producer rarely makes their own base spirit. Instead they buy a neutral spirit and then re-distill it with a selection of botanicals in order to achieve a flavor that they like.

The word *gin* comes from the Dutch word for *juniper*, so it stands to reason that gin will taste predominantly of that. Other common botanicals include coriander, cardamom, citrus peel, licorice, angelica, and orris, to name a scant few. Some producers go very heavy on the juniper—Tanqueray being an example—whereas others favor different botanicals.

Gin is a huge category with a ton of diversity, which makes cocktail development around this spirit tricky because what works with one gin does not always work for another. The safest bet is to find a London dry gin, so named in contrast to the sweetened gins that preceded its appearance in the 1830s. Great examples of this style are Tanqueray, Beefeater, and Sipsmith. If you delve into smaller producers, especially newer ones that are trying out more innovative botanicals—such as Greenhook, made with ginger and chamomile—you'll find they do not always work in every situation.

Absinthe

Technically, absinthe is similar to gin in that it's a base of neutral spirit with botanicals added. It's a common misconception that absinthe is a liqueur, but unlike liqueurs, absinthe is generally bottled without sweetener. It is, however, bottled at an extremely high ABV, usually around 60%, so very few people drink it straight.* Lots of recipes call for it as a modifier, which means you're adding only a small measure in order to contribute an intriguing dimension to a drink.

Classically, absinthe is flavored with wormwood, fennel, and anise. Some more modern producers, like St. George, add additional botanicals like hyssop and lemon balm. Wormwood is intensely bitter. Fennel and anise are sweeter but are generally not loved by Americans, most of whom did not grow up with their licorice-like flavor and thereby learn to love it.

Let's get this out of the way: People think absinthe makes you hallucinate.

---

* Although I can't say I haven't done it.

It does not. There is a compound in wormwood, *thujone*, that has a similar molecular structure to THC, but it has none of the effects. At very high doses it could give you a seizure, but there's thujone in many things we eat, like sage, and I haven't heard of any sage seizures. Absinthe developed this dangerous image because it was popular in the 1870s with artsy-fartsy Parisian weirdos—the gays, like Rimbaud and Oscar Wilde—and then was swept up in a moral panic and temperance movement in Europe in the early 1900s. Ultimately, thanks to a high-profile murder case out of Switzerland known as the Absinthe Murders (look it up, it's amazing), absinthe was declared illegal. It wasn't legalized in the United States until 2007.

LIQUEURS

Liqueurs are a central element of the drink maker's tool kit. They are some of the best ways to preserve and include flavors in cocktails. Liqueurs are made from a base of neutral alcohol infused[*] with various fruits, herbs, cocoa, etc., to which sugar is then added to reach the necessary sweetness level. Their ABV is usually lower than that of base spirits, but sometimes it's as high or higher. There is a legal definition for how much sugar a liqueur must have, but unless you're looking to create your own, all you need to know is that liqueurs are sweet.

Some liqueurs that you should keep in your home bar at all times are an orange liqueur such as Cointreau, Grand Marnier, or blue curaçao (don't @ me); crème de cacao (chocolate); crème de framboise (raspberry); yellow and green Chartreuse (both herbal and slightly bitter); St-Germain (elderflower); Luxardo Maraschino (cherry); Luxardo Amaretto (almond); and the infamous melon liqueur Midori (also don't @ me). Lejay is the only crème de cassis producer I acknowledge.

Amaro

Amaros[†] are bitter liqueurs. Most are from Italy, but you can find them from all over the world.

Amaros can provide a ton of complexity in cocktails and are fabulous on their own as well. (A simple amaro Highball is a fantastic apéritif or lunchtime drink.) Amaro is usually made with a base of neutral spirit that's macerated with botanicals such as gentian, Chinese rhubarb, orange peel, vanilla, clove, and saffron. The bitterness of each individual amaro can vary, but they all share this core trait.

A good introduction to amaro is to start off with something light and relatively less bitter, like Amaro

---

[*] Alternatively, you can say "macerated" if you like using words that sound like "masturbated."

[†] In the original Italian, *amaro* is spelled *amari* in the plural, and some people use this when speaking English. I find this to be a needless and pompous complication, so I abide by the standard English convention of pluralizing words with an *s*. Deal with it.

Montenegro, Cardamaro, or Aperol, and then graduate to more intense stuff like Cynar, Zucca Rabarbaro, Braulio, and Averna, before ending on brutes like Fernet-Branca and Elisir Novosalus.

In cocktails, amaro is an excellent addition and can even be used as a base. It's important to keep balance in mind, though. While amaros are balanced on their own, they can be a bully in cocktails and overpower the other ingredients you're working with, so you always want to be judicious with their use and take a less-is-more approach.

BITTERS

Cocktail bitters are a little bit like more concentrated versions of amaro. I know this is kind of an irresponsible oversimplification, but it's a useful shorthand. The two contain many of the same ingredients and serve similar functions, but you need to use only a few drops/dashes of bitters to achieve a balanced cocktail.

There are three types of bitters that you should concern yourself with: Angostura, Peychaud's, and orange. Yes, of course there is a plenitude of other bitters out there, but if you want to stock your bar with classics that you will use over and over, get these.

Angostura's recipe is a secret, but I can detect clove, cinnamon, and gentian. These are the bitters you'll probably use the most often. Peychaud's

is from New Orleans and its predominant flavor is anise. It is made bitter with gentian. Angostura also makes orange bitters—flavored, unsurprisingly, with bitter orange peel. While you can find orange bitters from a few different producers, Angostura's works best in the widest array of applications.

FORTIFIED AND AROMATIZED WINES

I'm lumping a lot of very different liquids into this category, but what unites them all is that they're made from a base of wine that's "fortified" with small amounts of alcohol, and in some cases botanicals. Some might not even call them spirits in the strict sense of the word—this is hair-splitting as far as we're concerned.

Vermouth is the most popular example of a fortified and aromatized wine. Dry vermouth is more commonly associated with France. It has a light straw color and is flavored with gentian, chamomile, and bitter orange, among other things. My favorite dry vermouth is Dolin Dry. Originating in northern Italy, sweet vermouth is usually a rusty cola-brown color and is commonly flavored with vanilla, saffron, and bitter orange. My two favorites are Carpano Antica and Cocchi Vermouth di Torino. Vermouth is essentially wine and clocks in at around 17% to 20% ABV, so once you open it, you should to treat it the way you would an open bottle of wine.

Sherry is a fortified wine from Spain, made by adding a small amount of alcohol to wine and allowing it to undergo a secondary fermentation—essentially, controlled spoilage. Broadly speaking, sherries have high acidity and a complex nutty aroma. They are classified by dryness: Fino and Manzanilla are bone-dry, Oloroso and Palo Cortado are sweeter, while Pedro Ximénez is quite sweet. Sherry works nicely as a cocktail ingredient and can be an excellent source of acidity, especially as a substitute for vermouth in stirred cocktails.

NONALCOHOLIC INGREDIENTS

WATER

Water is everywhere, especially in cocktails. Spirits, juices, syrups, and so on all contain water to some degree. Unless you're making your own syrups (which I encourage you to do), you can't control the water sources in these indirect ways of adding water to a cocktail. You can, however, directly control the water content in your drinks in a few ways.

Flat Water

For flat water I suggest always using filtered tap water, including for making ice if you're using molds. Chlorine and other chemicals used to treat tap water can interfere with aromatics.

Bubbly Water

I'm a huge ho for sparkling water. I consider a kitchen fully stocked with various types of bubbly water to be a worthy indulgence. But not all sparkling water is the same.

When you're selecting a sparkling water for your cocktails, seltzer and soda water* are nice because they usually contain big, noticeable bubbles that hold up when you add them to cocktails. Vintage and Polar are my go-to brands. I prefer cans over bottles because once you open any vessel, the clock starts ticking on the carbonation, even if you close the cap super tight, and cans offer the smallest volume you can open at one time.[†]

Mineral waters can provide an elegant texture, thanks to the mineral content and generally less prominent bubbles, so they're a better choice if you want something more subtle and refined. They work nicely in Highball-type cocktails where the drink is made mostly of spirits and water. I like

---

*   Seltzer is straight water and CO_2 bubbles, while soda water contains sodium and other minerals. Although seltzer has a sharper texture than soda, they will work more or less interchangeably in cocktails.

†   Also, aluminum is more recyclable than plastic.

Pellegrino, Saratoga, and, if you want to get wild with minerality, Gerolsteiner.

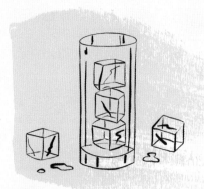

Ice

While I would not consider ice an ingredient in the formal cocktail-recipe sense, it is indeed a huge factor in the way your cocktails turn out. You can actually bifurcate its role into work ice and drink ice. The work ice is the unseen stuff you use to accomplish drink-producing tasks like chilling, dilution, and, in the case of shaken drinks, aeration. Drink ice is the seen stuff that goes in drinks.

Work ice does not have to be pretty, as it just serves as a means to technical ends. It has to be big enough so that it does not totally break apart or melt too quickly during shaking and stirring, so one-inch-by-one-inch-ish cubes are ideal. If you don't have an ice machine, get a few small ice molds, though I recommend buying ice if you're making more than a couple of drinks.

With drink ice you have to be a bit more careful if you really want to make a nice cocktail and impress someone. If you don't give a shit, which I frequently do not, you can use whatever work ice you're using as drink ice. If you want to get fancy, buy big two-inch-square ice molds, or, if you want to get *really* fancy, buy dead-clear cubes from an ice purveyor. It doesn't hurt to do a quick web search to see if there's an ice sculptor around who will make you cubes. Buy a bunch and keep them in your freezer (sealed tight to prevent frosting) and you have pretty ice to bust out whenever you want. It's a high-value way to impress the shit out of someone (if you feel like it).

TONIC WATER

I *love* tonic water. If I could pull off an Oprah "I love bread!" video but with tonic water, I would.[*]

I developed a taste for tonic water when I was in college. When I would visit my parents at home in the summer, we would have gin and tonics. My mom would make them in these pretty blue and white glasses with tons of ice, tons of Tanqueray, and tons of tonic water. It wasn't even good tonic water, but the emotional experience convinced me that the taste of tonic water was a good one. The flavor of tonic water comes from quinine, which is derived from the bark

---

[*]   I just might still. . . .

of the cinchona tree; the cinchona tree is native to the Andes and its bark is an antimalarial as well as a muscle relaxant. Quinine will kill you at high doses, but so will everything.

Many tonic waters are good enough to act as a stand-alone beverage. Fever-Tree, Q, East Imperial, and the Whole Foods 365 brand are my favorites.

JUICES

Lemon and Lime Juice

Extremely high acidity and relative lack of sugar make lemon and lime juice a great way to incorporate acidity into your drinks and balance out sweetness. There is some mystical difference between lemon and lime juice, and some drinks just work with one or the other; there is no hard-and-fast rule, as far as I can tell. That said, lemon juice does tend to be a bit rounder, tasting more of orange, whereas lime is a bit sharper, with slight hints of green apple skins.

Unfortunately, lemon and lime juice are quite fragile and oxidize quickly, after which they taste funky and metallic. They are best within 12 hours of juicing, up to 36 is okay, and you can even go a few days if you keep the juice in the fridge, but don't expect to wow anyone at that point. You'd be surprised how the difference between a fine drink and a life-changing one is just a matter of fresh citrus juice. You'll probably end up using more than you expected—I almost always run out of lemon or lime juice if I'm serving drinks at home—so plan to make a little more than you think you'll need, just in case.

Grapefruit Juice

Grapefruit juice doesn't have the same concentration of acidity as lemon or lime, so most drinks will rely on grapefruit juice alongside another source. Aromatically, I find grapefruit to be the most interesting of the basic citruses, and the hit of bitterness adds a degree of sophistication. I always go for red grapefruit, though if it's unavailable, you can use white as well. Ripeness levels can also vary, but not so much that you need to tweak your recipe every time you use grapefruit juice, but be aware.

Yuzu Juice

Yuzu juice is a great bar pantry staple. The fruit is native to East Asia; it grows rampant all over Japan. The winter when I lived in Kyoto, I would go running along the Kamo River and I could just reach up and grab one and eat it if I was feeling depleted. The aromatics of yuzu are intense. To me, it's like a melon-y Meyer lemon with a hint of tangerine.

Fresh yuzu fruit is nearly impossible to find in the United States, especially on the East Coast. Best case is if you go to a specialty shop you might be able to find two gnarled and juiceless knobs that have the audacity to call themselves yuzu. Instead, look for bottled yuzu juice. It's readily available online, but all the juice is pasteurized so it has some of that staleness that you find in too-old citrus juices. But that's okay, because a little goes a long way (and can easily overpower your drinks if you're not careful). It lasts quite a long time in the fridge and you can even freeze it.

A word of warning: it is *very* easy to buy salted yuzu juice—don't. Pay close attention to the label; be sure that it says "100% Yuzu Juice" and that salt is not listed anywhere on the label. There is not much variation between brands, but the Yakami Orchard brand is fairly ubiquitous online.

Pineapple Juice

I really grapple with the store-bought vs. DIY question here. Plain ol' grocery store canned pineapple juice is consistent and can really go the distance in cocktails, especially where you're not relying on a ton of it, but there is a special freshness and life to recently juiced pineapple. However, it's hard to find consistent ripeness with pineapples; they ripen unevenly from the bottom up. Also, juicing pineapple is a pain in the ass. I don't have a fancy juicer, so I purée my pineapple in the blender and then pour it through a fine-mesh strainer. Whether you choose DIY or store-bought, pineapple juice imparts a lush honeyed quality to cocktails, and when shaken, it provides a great foamy texture.

Cranberry Juice

Cranberry juice suffers from a misrepresentation problem. Yes, the

Ocean Spray stuff is tasty, but it's more like frankenberry juice: mostly apple juice with some cranberry flavor and a lot of added sugar. The best way to make real cranberry juice is to buy the stuff labeled "100% Juice" that you can find in stores pretty easily, or online. It is nearly undrinkably acidic on its own, so you must mix it with simple syrup (see page 68) in equal parts. This version of cranberry juice will give you pure cranberry flavors, bright acidity, and a noticeable supply of tannins, which are the compounds found in wine that impart a grippy, astringent texture. Once blended, this mixture will keep in the fridge for up to a month, or you can freeze it for up to six months.

Watermelon Juice

Watermelon juice is great to use in refreshing summer cocktails. However, it's extremely fragile and goes stale quickly, so you want to make the juice right before you use it. If you don't have a juicer, just purée the melon pulp (minus seeds) in a blender or food processor and then pour it through a fine-mesh strainer. Watermelon is one of the most iconic summer flavors, providing a roundness without an overpowering amount of sweetness.

Verjus

Verjus comes from the juice of unripe wine grapes and is one of the ways I like to incorporate acidity into cocktails without having to go through the rigmarole of juicing citrus. What's

more, it is highly useful when it comes to alcohol-free cocktails, as it lends a mature sensibility that's reminiscent of wine. Unopened bottles will last months if not years, and once opened, verjus will keep in the fridge for at least three weeks. My favorite is from Wöllfer Estate, but there are many good brands out there.

SWEETENERS

Simple Syrup

This staple ingredient is made up of water and sugar. In order to incorporate sugar into your cocktails, you need to dissolve it into something; you'll end up with a grainy mess if you try to just put dry sugar in your mixing tin or shaker because the sugar will not dissolve in time. You can buy simple syrup, but it's also quite easy to make yourself (see page 68).

Agave Nectar

People try to say that agave nectar is better for you than plain sugar, but it's not—it's still sugar. Agave nectar brings in some of the roasted, deeper flavors of the cooked plant, so it's nice to use in cocktails that contain agave spirits because it tends to highlight that flavor. Agave nectar on its own has a hard time dissolving into cocktails, so dilute it with water (see page 84) before using.

Honey

Honey is a great sweetener because it never goes bad. You can't just use straight honey in a cocktail, however. Like agave nectar, it won't readily integrate with the other ingredients and will end up glued to the bottom of your shaker, so you need to dilute it (see page 186). From an aromatic standpoint, honey can be overpowering, but it's compatible with a wide variety of ingredients, so it's fun to play around with.

Maple Syrup

Maple syrup is another buy-it-and-forget-it sweetener that's great to have around. Unlike honey, it doesn't need to be diluted with water in order for it to integrate well into cocktails. I always prefer Grade B, sometimes referred to as "Grade A: Dark Amber," because it has a richer flavor and dissolves more readily. My love of Grade B maple syrup was kindled when I worked at PDT, serving the Benton's Old Fashioned, made from bacon-infused bourbon and Grade B maple syrup. It's one of the most perfect cocktails out there.

Demerara

My favorite sugar is demerara sugar. It's an unrefined sugar that still has most of the molasses remaining, so it has the full flavor range of sugarcane, as opposed to the nonaromatic sweetness of regular refined sugar. As a syrup (see page 72), it's great with barrel-aged spirits and is the best sweetener to use in an Old Fashioned.

Black Sugar

Actually, just kidding: my favorite sugar is black sugar, or *kurozato*. It's made in Okinawa and has an intense earthy, smoky flavor. It sometimes comes in syrup form, but most likely you'll find it in lumpy cubes. You can straight up eat them like candy if you hate your pancreas, or you can make a syrup out of them (see page 208).

Ginger Syrup

This syrup (see page 106) is a pain in the ass to make but it is so worth it. It's the best way to incorporate the zing from ginger into cocktails, and due to its high sugar content, it can stay fresh in the fridge for a long time, and even longer if you freeze it.

Grenadine

Grenadine is simple syrup made with pomegranate juice instead of water (see page 129). It's one of my favorite ways to add a distinctive hit of sweetness, acidity, and juicy aromatics to a cocktail. Luckily, it can be swapped out perfectly with simple syrup without your having to adjust the original recipe, because the sweetness and acidity are balanced.

Infused Syrups

We can take leafy herbs like basil, mint, and tarragon, as well as fruits like raspberries, and blend them into simple syrup (or into honey or agave syrup, for that matter). It's a good way to preserve fresh ingredients, especially those that have a limited season, like strawberries. Infusing syrups is a great solution whenever you have, for instance, more basil than you know what to do with.

Cane Syrup

Sometimes you'll see this listed as "Sirop de Canne," the French spelling, because a fair number of cane syrups come from Martinique, a former French colony. Cane syrup is made from sugarcane juice with some of the water evaporated. I love cane syrup. It comes premade and keeps forever without refrigeration. It provides a lovely lush texture to shaken drinks like daiquiris. Just keep in mind: its sweetness is a little more concentrated than that of simple syrup.

Orgeat

First off, it's pronounced like a French word, *oar-JAH*. Second, it's a delicious, fragrant Middle Eastern syrup made from apricot kernels or almonds (they taste similar). Most orgeats also contain some kind of floral essence, like orange-flower water. There are two types of orgeat: industrial, which contains a fair amount of preservatives but has kind of a classic taste and sweetness level, or artisanal stuff that tastes more like almonds and is less sweet. Older cocktail recipes are based on the industrial stuff, and due to the widening availability of fancy, gentrified orgeat, recipes developed more recently will depend on the less sweet version. All of the recipes in this book are based on the latter.

Preserves

Honestly, I get super stressed out when I do not have a jar or two of Bonne Maman preserves in my fridge. Another bar pantry staple, unopened preserves keep indefinitely, and once opened they'll keep in the fridge for a very long time. They're useful for adding a hit of sweetness and acidity, as well as fruit aromatics, to cocktails, but keep in mind that if you're using any additional sources of acidity or sweetness, you'll need to adjust in order to get the balance right.

MILK

Lots of great drinks call for milk, and good milk is important to me. Milk supplies flavor and texture, and its fats and proteins help smooth rough edges. When shaken, milk froths up generously, creating a nice airy texture. To me, cheap milk tastes like sadness and cow mucus, so I prefer the fancy grass-fed organic stuff. (Though if you're in a pinch, the cheap stuff is not going to ruin your drinks.)

EGGS

Eggs provide protein that creates a matrix that holds air and flavors. Go for the nice stuff if you can, especially if you are making whole-egg drinks. The flavor from the yolks is far superior with pasture-raised chickens that are allowed to eat bugs, which imparts more carotene—and flavor—into the yolks. Cooped-up corn-fed chickens are deficient in it. Raw eggs are often shunned due to concerns about food safety.[*] Don't be afraid—the inclusion of raw eggs in your repertoire will not only expand the number of drinks you can make, it will also expand your capabilities, as eggs can provide textures and flavors like no other ingredient can.

---

[*] Raw spinach has a much higher risk of salmonella, and yet many people have no problem chowing down on raw spinach on a daily basis.

Egg whites alone will still provide an airy texture, but you won't get the heavy richness that comes with the yolk. Use egg whites when making brighter drinks with citrus, such as a whiskey sour (page 95), and whole eggs for heavier, fuller cocktails like eggnog (page 165).

GARNISHES

Citrus Wheels

These primarily serve a visual purpose, but like a wedge, they can provide slightly juicier aromatics to a drink. A properly made citrus wheel is de-seeded (see page 50), with only a small slice made through the skin on one side of the fruit so that the structure of the wheel holds it in place when perched on a glass.*

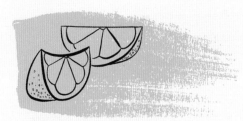

Citrus Wedges

Citrus wedges invite the drinker to squeeze them into the drink before drinking. For example, a properly made gin and tonic is really lacking without some kind of citrus, but it's a little unceremonious to splash straight juice in there, so we put a lime wedge on the rim of the glass to get that hit of acidity, plus aromatics from the peel, right before we start drinking. Refer to the illustrations on page 50 for a step-by-step on how to make a citrus wedge.

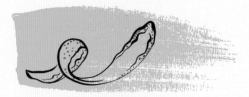

Citrus Peels

Citrus peels are by far the most ubiquitous and effective cocktail garnish. Lemon, orange, and grapefruit peels smell amazing and can support a drink's existing aromatics or provide a vibrant contrast. I'm kinda meh on lime peels—they don't smell that great. Sorry, limes. If you have access to fancy citrus like Meyer lemons, mandarins, pomelos, and the like, you can get even more creative.

---

* PLEASE, FOR THE LOVE OF ALL THAT IS PURE AND GOOD IN THIS WORLD, MAKE SURE YOU'VE DE-SEEDED YOUR LEMON WHEELS AND WEDGES BEFORE SERVING THEM. THERE IS NO EXCUSE FOR NOT DOING THIS. ALL IT TAKES IS A FEW FLICKS OF THE KNIFE TO PUSH THEM OUT.

Thank you for coming to my TED Talk.

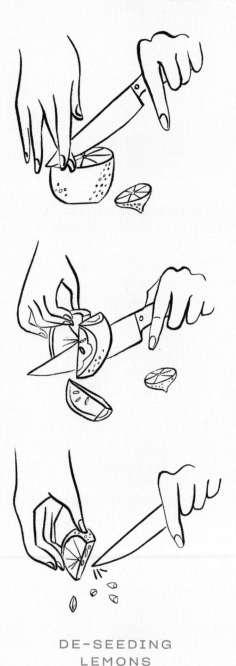

DE-SEEDING
LEMONS

Citrus peels contain aromatic essential oils that, when expressed over the top of a cocktail, will create an aromatic cloud over the drink, which is the first thing someone smells when they bring the glass to their face. The cloud is then followed by the aromatics from the cocktail itself, giving the drinker a more layered and complex experience.

Always, always wash the whole citrus with soap and water before using it.

Cherries

Cocktail cherries are awesome, but not the radioactive bright red ones. Actually, fuck it, those are great, too—there's a time and a place for everything. The most delicious cherries are made by Luxardo, and they come in a can or bottle and can easily be found online or in specialty food shops. You can drop the cherries in the drink or put them on a toothpick. Up to you and your mood.

Aromatic Sprays

I know how precious it might seem, but it's a really good idea to have an atomizer to spray highly aromatic liquids like absinthe over a drink. Doing so serves the same purpose as citrus peel garnishes: it applies an added layer of complexity that sits on top of the drink. You can play with the spatial arrangements of aromatics much more deliberately with the help of a spray bottle.

Equipment

GLASSWARE

It is generally regarded as standard practice to pour beverages into something other than their original containers before consuming them. Aside from literally drinking rum out of the bottle at 7:00 a.m., there are reasonable exceptions to this, and we will get to them.

If you're going to be semi-serious about home bartending, I recommend using water to measure the real volumes of all the glasses you have on hand; this will make it easier to select the appropriate one in any given scenario.

Keep your glassware at room temperature most of the time, but pop the glasses in the freezer twenty minutes before serving. It's important to chill glassware so that when you pour a properly chilled drink, the glass does not warm it up. If you leave glasses in the freezer permanently,

not only do they take up space, they're also likely to break.

Coupe

The coupe, also known as a cocktail glass, is the gold standard for cocktail glassware. It should be large enough to hold a 5-ounce drink and have a curved bowl that helps keep the liquid inside. (This is opposed to the satanic martini glass, which no one in their right mind should ever use.) Some coupes are deeper and more cupped, while others are more saucer-y.* The coupe has a stem, which allows you to hold the drink without the heat of your hand transferring to the drink and warming it up. The skin on your fingers is thin and has more nerve endings and blood vessels than other parts of your body, making it a great heat transfer point. Keeping that away from your drink is important if you want it to stay cool as long as possible, which you should.

Use coupes for any drink served without ice, like daiquiris and martinis.

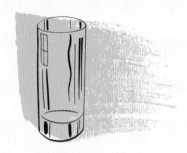

Collins/Highball

Larger glassware such as Collins and highball glasses are meant to hold larger drinks made with sparkling water, like gin and tonics and Highballs. Technically a Collins glass is a bit taller and has more capacity than a highball, but for our purposes, we can consider them in the same breath. And by "our purposes," I mean forgetting about them. They're kinda not necessary. If you have access to nice highball or Collins glasses, good for you. Otherwise feel free to use a standard water glass from your kitchen, or an old fashioned glass. Water glasses tend to be a bit larger and wider than highball/Collins glasses, but they're far more versatile.

Old Fashioned

If the coupe is the queen, then the old fashioned glass, also referred to as a rocks glass, is the king—or maybe vice versa. The best size is around 12 ounces. This gives you enough room for ice plus a full-size cocktail. If I had to pick only a single type of glassware to have in my bar, I would go with these. Use them to serve Old Fashioneds (duh) and on-the-rocks margaritas, but feel free to serve ice-less drinks in them as well if you don't feel like fumbling with a delicate coupe.

---

* I like the deeper ones. Giggidy.

Wine Glass

You should have some nice wine glasses in your house. I recommend a set of white wine glasses that can act as all-purpose. Wine glasses are a fine alternative to Collins glasses when you're making larger drinks that also contain ice—think spritzes—and can also be used in the place of coupes in a pinch. Don't bother with Champagne flutes. I find them unnecessary, and their tiny diameter limits the amount of aromatics that waft up from your drink—an important part of the sensory experience.

Tiki Glasses

I love tiki drinks and the mugs they come in. I also find most tiki iconography to be a racist pastiche of Pacific Island cultures along with some Caribbean elements bafflingly tossed in. But the fact remains that these vessels serve a worthy purpose. You can get *Game of*

Thrones- or even *My Little Pony*-themed tiki glasses to avoid the problematic nature of classic tiki iconography. You can find them in an astonishing variety of shapes, and they're usually huge, around 18 ounces; this means you can make big drinks.* Additionally, you don't have to look at what's inside. Most tiki drinks are a blend of many ingredients, sometimes resulting in an unappetizing muddy-brown hue. So you can sip your drink from an opaque Yoda tiki mug as you try to forget the fact that when we die, every thought and feeling we've ever had will be irreversibly lost to nothingness for all eternity.

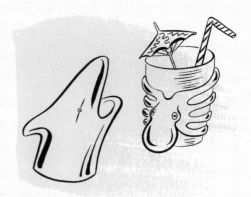

Mugs

I suspect you already have mugs around your home for tea and coffee. I also suspect you have only one of each type of mug. No one has matching mugs, and this really bothers me and I know it shouldn't. No one buys one

---

* Which I like because I like big drinks and I cannot lie.

plate at a time, but I have yet to visit a house where there was any kind of consistent coffee mug program. Yeah, that's right, I said coffee mug program.* Mugs are useful for hot drinks because the ceramic they're made of is not overly conductive and the handle prevents you from burning yourself, but you already knew this. The whole reason I'm including coffee mugs in my section on glassware is so that I could include a rant about how no one has matching coffee mugs. Thanks for reading.

TOOLS

There's a huge world of bar tools out there that you're free to spend a ton of money on, but you'd be surprised how little you can get by on with a bit of ingenuity. The following is my list of essentials, in order of their essential-ness. If you're just starting out, prioritize the tools at the beginning of this list and work your way through as your commitment to making drinks grows.

Shaking Tin Set

You want a shaking set with two metal parts: a large tumbler and a smaller one. A set that uses a pint glass tumbler is acceptable, but you should avoid it if possible. I like the all-metal Koriko brand for its build quality, but you can find other sets for dirt cheap. No matter how nice you go, they will always get dinged up from use. At home, you probably won't be using your shakers hundreds of times per day like in a bar, but even so, you might have to replace them every few years if you care about having perfect shiny shaking tins. I have a shitty set I don't care about and a nice set I bust out for special occasions.

---

* I'll be the first person to tell you that I'm a pretentious dick.

Jiggers

If you're making drinks at home, your bar set should include two jiggers: one that measures 1 ounce on one side and 2 on the other; and another that has ½-ounce and ¾-ounce measures. With these, you can pretty much measure all the standard pours that cocktail recipes call for.

My favorite small jigger is from Cocktail Kingdom; I get my big jigger from Barproducts.com.

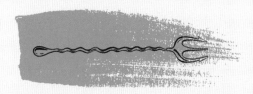

Barspoons / Chopsticks

Fancy people like to have fancy barspoons to stir their drinks, and that's fine. I have accumulated a ton of barspoons over the years, but I almost always stir my drinks with a large chopstick. A small one works great, too. It's actually easier to use a chopstick because you don't have to contend with the spoon part of it. You won't find recipes calling for a "barspoon"

measure in this book because it's pretty imprecise. I prefer to convert the measure to ⅛ ounce and use the small jigger instead.

Strainer

Every new bartender is told they need to use two different strainers: julep for stirred drinks and Hawthorne for shaken drinks. You can use the Hawthorne for both shaken and stirred drinks, so there is absolutely no functional reason why you need a julep strainer in your life. My favorite strainer is the OXO SteeL cocktail strainer.

Knives

If you are at all serious about doing anything in your kitchen, you owe it to yourself to have at least one really good knife that you have professionally sharpened on a regular basis. A sharp knife is safer to use and will allow you to do more cool stuff with your ingredients, like making very thin slices of stuff for garnishes and so on. It's a big commitment, but throwing down for a chef's knife made by Shun or Wüsthof is definitely worth it. Alternatively, if I'm traveling, I like to have a couple of small, cheap knives from Kuhn Rikon to throw in my tool bag; they work great.

Juicers

Electric juicers are fine, especially if you're doing a large volume of juicing. If you're planning on any mobile bartending, get a small hand juicer that you can take with you. Juicing is a pain in the ass and there is no tool that will make it not that. Just try to find a juicing method that works for you. However you do it, make absolutely sure to strain out all the seeds and pulp before using the juice in cocktails.

Peeler

I buy three-packs of cheapo Y-shape peelers and toss them when they get dull. Three should last you a good long while. Don't waste money on a fancy vegetable peeler. The blade will get dull and there's really no way to sharpen it.

Tea Strainer

Use a tea strainer when you want to fine-strain. By that, I mean eliminate any extra bits from your drinks, like pieces of muddled fruit or herbs, or ice chips. You can also use it to strain seeds and pulp from your citrus juice. The Coco Strainer from Cocktail Kingdom is great.

Spray Bottle/Atomizer

Many recipes call for rinses and floats, and a spray bottle is the way to efficiently accomplish these tasks. Misto is my favorite, but in a pinch you can find cheaper atomizers online—just don't store anything in them long-term, as the plastic ones will retain flavors permanently.

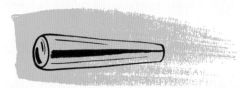

Muddler

If you're making drinks with any solid ingredients that you need to break up—like fruits, vegetables, or a dry sugar cube—you need a muddler. There are a lot of surprisingly useless muddlers out there, but the best one is the Bad Ass Muddler, created by my dear friend and mentor Don Lee and sold by Cocktail Kingdom. It's made out of food-grade plastic and it's heavy enough that you can literally kill someone with it. I can also tell you it's a fantastic dildo.

Cambros

Here begins my love letter to Cambros. Chances are, if you've never worked in a bar or restaurant, you have no idea what a Cambro is. Cambro is a manufacturing company with all kinds of products; when I say "Cambro" I mean their CamSquare containers specifically. These containers are superior to any amateur kitchen bullshit out there: they're sturdier, cheaper, stack better, have better seals, come in a huge variety of sizes, and you can pour from them surprisingly well. They can even serve as a cocktail shaker in a pinch (if you want to shake up ten cocktails at a time—do you).

You can find them online at Webstaurantstore.com and I suggest getting a few of the 2- and 4-quart sizes with lids.

Deli Containers

Yes, I am talking about those cylindrical hazy plastic containers that come with your restaurant food deliveries. It is perfectly noble to build a stockpile based on past orders, but it's actually very practical to order an unused set online and forget about it forever. Ideally get three sizes: cup (8 ounces), pint (16 ounces), and quart (32 ounces). The added value of these containers is that they also serve as measuring cups in a wide variety of less-than-ideal situations, and you can even use them as a shaking set if you're desperate. When I talk about airtight containers in recipes in this book, this is what I'm referring to.

Gold Coffee Filters

These filters have an extremely fine mesh that's great for filtering out small particles from juices, infusions, syrups, and so on. They fit nicely on top of a quart-size deli container as well. They could even work as a cocktail strainer in a pinch.

Big Ice Molds

You'll need big molds to make big blocks of sexy drink ice. There are a bunch out there and none is that much better than the other as long as you go with ones made from silicone because they will last longer and are easier to work with. When it comes time to remove ice from the mold, let the ice thaw a bit before removing the cubes; otherwise you damage the molds by forcing the ice out before it's ready and ripping the silicone.

Fancy Bitters Bottles

I debated whether to include these as bar basics, but they can serve an important purpose if you really care about the precise amounts of bitters in your drinks. Most cocktail recipes you come across that call for bitters will use the measurement "dash" to indicate how much to add. The problem with this is that the term "dash" refers to a physical action of dashing a bitters bottle, and not to any kind of objective volume. The size of the dash will depend on a lot of factors: the size of the bottle, the fullness of the bottle, how big the hole is at the top of the bottle.

This is all to say that the dash is an unreliable and quite variable way to measure bitters. To remedy this, you can get little glass bottles that help standardize many of the aforementioned variables. The only trade-off is that the dash sizes are nowhere near the sizes that come out of, say, a half-full 12-ounce Angostura bottle. To account for this discrepancy, if you're using fancy bottles, I recommend doubling the written amount in the recipe you're using—all the recipes in this book are based on dashes from the original vessel.

Mixing Glass

A fancy mixing glass is a nice thing to have, but it is very, very optional. You don't need one to stir drinks. In situations where I don't care how I look, I use the small tin of the shaking set. I do have some nice mixing glasses if I'm looking to impress, but they don't see the light of day too often because I don't need to fucking impress anybody.

Techniques

MEASURE

The first step in making a cocktail is measuring the ingredients. You want to make sure every ingredient you put into the cocktail is measured precisely and accurately. Unless you don't want to, in which case you still want to "measure" in some loose sense of the word. This was a really convoluted way for me to introduce you to the concept of jiggering and its nemesis, free pouring.

Jiggering is important when you want to produce precise, consistent cocktails. When you're working with recipes that call for a quarter and sometimes ⅛ of an ounce, jiggering is nonnegotiable. When filling a jigger completely, you'll pour liquid in it until the surface tension keeps a bubble hovering over the top. This is a foolproof and objective way to know you've measured accurately.

If a recipe has larger measurements, and ingredients that won't overpower the drink if you use a little too much, you can free-pour, which is exactly what it sounds like. Highballs and gin and tonics, for example, can be free-poured. Still, I recommend that you jigger them at first, to get the hang of the balance.

SHAKE AND STIR

Once you've measured your ingredients, you need to mix, chill, and dilute them, and in the case of certain drinks, you also want to aerate them.

To accomplish all four of these tasks, you shake. To shake a cocktail, measure all of the ingredients into the smaller shaker tin, then fill it all the way with ice. Close the large tin on top, pick it up, flip it over so that the large tin is on the bottom, and shake. You want to use one hand on each end of the shaker to hold the set securely, and to keep the two pieces together while you shake the living shit out of your drink.

SHAKE AND STIR

When I say shake the living shit out of it, I mean it. A wimpy, noncommittal shake is the death of countless cocktails, night after night, all over the world. Great shaken cocktails require you to shake as hard as you possibly can for fifteen seconds. I highly recommend setting a stopwatch so you can get an understanding of what fifteen seconds really is—it's a lot longer than you think. This intensity and duration is necessary to get the drink ridiculously cold and ridiculously frothy.

So what about drinks that only need to be mixed, chilled, and diluted? The dividing line between shaken drinks and stirred drinks is generally drawn at citrus and eggs. Anything without these two ingredients generally only needs to be stirred. Stirring is a gentler process: the ice stays intact, no air is incorporated, and the drink doesn't get quite as cold or as diluted.

The key to stirring is to gently move the ice and ingredients around for fifteen to twenty seconds in either the small shaking tin or a mixing glass. Be careful not to slosh, as doing so will incorporate air bubbles as well as cause the ice to chip and melt quickly, risking over-dilution.

STRAIN

Once you've sufficiently mixed, chilled, diluted, and, in the case of shaken drinks, aerated your drink, you need a way to separate that drink from the work ice. Enter: the strainer.

In the case of a stirred drink, this task is pretty straightforward: place the strainer on the rim of the mixing vessel and pour the cocktail into your desired glassware.

But there is an added concern when dealing with shaken drinks. Because of the violence of the shaking process, the work ice gets broken into pieces of varying size. A certain contingent of people like fine ice chips in their shaken drinks, and I am one of them. I think they offer a nice texture and make the drink feel more alive. To accomplish this, you perform a technique known as "closing the gate," meaning you place a bit of added pressure downward to reduce the opening between the rim of the shaker and the edge of the strainer. Doing so will keep the bigger chunks out while letting the fine bits through. If you're the kind of person who likes drinks without ice chips (I get it), then fine-strain your shaken drinks. My default is to close the gate, and I recommend that every shaken drink made in this book should be strained this way.

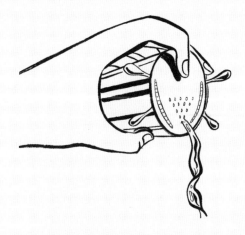

CLOSING THE GATE

FINE-STRAIN

FINE-STRAIN

Fine-straining is what happens when you hold a small tea strainer under the flow from the shaker in order to capture all the ice bits coming through. If you have any drinks, shaken or stirred, with muddled ingredients like fruit or herbs that you don't want in the drink (and you don't want any), then you need to fine-strain your drink. Although you won't have fine ice chips as a result. Like many things in life, it's a trade-off.

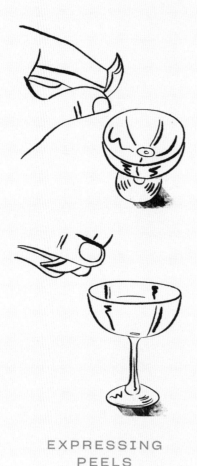

EXPRESSING
PEELS

DRY SHAKE

If a recipe tells you to dry shake, it means to combine all your ingredients in a shaker, shake without ice briefly—five seconds tops—*then* add ice and shake for fifteen seconds as normal. This technique is used primarily when there is an egg product in the cocktail. The proteins in the eggs unfold to create a matrix with the air and give the drink its proper texture. Some people suggest dry shaking when there is any dairy such as cream or milk, but I don't find it necessary.

RINSE

Rinsing a glass means you should pour a trace amount of something intensely aromatic—think absinthe or an amaro—into the glass before pouring the rest of the ingredients into the glass. You can accomplish this by pouring a tiny amount in the glass, rotating it around to coat the inside, and discarding any excess. Alternatively, you can spray the inside of the glass using an atomizer.

EXPRESSING PEELS

Citrus peel contains aromatic oils. Expressing it over the surface of a drink gives the drinker a bright, fruity prelude to the rest of the experience. Holding the peel five to six inches above the drink, spray the oils over the drink's surface by gently pinching together the long edges of the strip of peel so that the oils rest on top of the drink. You'll see some people wringing the peel out and then smooshing the skin around the surface of the drink as if the oils were precious, life-giving manna. Don't do this. The whole point is to create a subtle layer of oils over the top of the drink, not to saturate the whole thing with citrus oil, especially since some of the oils on the skin are bitter and will mess up the drink's balance.

PERCHING ON THE RIM

Once you've expressed the peel, it's nice to adorn the rim of the glass with that peel to reinforce the presence of the invisible cloud of aromatic oils. To perch a peel, cut a one-inch slit in the center of the peel and slide that onto the rim. I prefer this method to simply dropping the peel in the drink, or laying it on top, because it holds the peel securely and keeps it from drifting into your mouth when you take a sip.

FAT WASH

This is a fancy term for infusing the flavor of fats into spirits. The technique uses the solvent properties of alcohol to strip aromatic molecules from the fat.* You don't need any fancy lab equipment—just a freezer and a filter. To fat wash, simply combine a spirit and a flavorful fat such as butter, coconut oil, or even an animal fat, let them infuse overnight, and then chill the mixture to separate and solidify the leftover fat. Lastly, remove the solidified fat.

Once you get the hang of it, there is an endless combination of fats and spirits you can play with, in anything from a gimlet to an Old Fashioned. Use the recipe for the Coconut Old Fashioned on page 145 as a template to riff.

PERCHING ON
THE RIM

---

* Substrate Transfer is my drag name.

FEELING OBJECTIVE

The nine drinks in this chapter represent the most elemental of cocktail recipes. They form the foundation upon which almost all other objectively delicious cocktails are based—so it's a good idea to really get these down. Understanding these drinks will go a long way toward making you feel confident as you expand your repertoire; you can always fall back on them as long as you know why they work. Don't worry, I'm going to tell you why they work objectively, and I'm also going to tell you which other drinks in this book trace their lineage back to each archetype to help you begin to understand riffing and modification.

I have conveniently placed a (kinda lengthy, sorry*) explanation for why these drinks work so well at the beginning of each recipe. Feel free to skip these intros if you just want to get down to making drinks. I totally honestly 100% won't be offended at all. Really.

* Not sorry.

Daiquiri

The daiquiri shows how even the very simplest cocktail can transcend its ingredients and magically become more than the sum of its parts. The acidity of lime juice and the flavors of rum are brought into delicious focus by being super fucking cold and slightly frothy—a result of diligent and vigorous shaking. A properly made daiquiri will taste like rum and limes . . . but will also taste like a daiquiri.

People might associate the daiquiri with unfortunate spring break experiences at all-inclusive resorts in Cancún, but it really is one of the most elegant and primal cocktails. Its simplicity is its greatest asset as well as its greatest weakness. With only three ingredients, there is very little room to hide flaws. You can fuck this drink up pretty easily: by using shitty rum, stale lime juice, or worse, sour mix, all of which taste terrible and will be very obvious in the drink.

Drinks that follow the formula of 2 ounces base spirit, ¾ ounce lemon or lime juice, and ¾ ounce sweetener are called sours, and this template can be riffed endlessly. I encourage you to play around with it—try using a blend of 1 ounce of dark rum and 1 ounce of white, or replace a ¼ or ½ ounce of the rum with something overproof (stronger than 40% ABV).

The daiquiri also works with pretty much any base spirit (make it with gin and it's a gimlet, and it's great made with Manzanilla sherry), and with any standard sweetener like honey syrup or agave, as well as infused simple syrups. There's a surprising amount of play in this one humble cocktail.

Makes 1 drink

2 ounces **rum**

¾ ounce **fresh lime juice**

¾ ounce **Simple Syrup** (recipe follows)

Optional Garnish Lime wheel

In a shaker, combine the drink ingredients. Add ice and shake vigorously for 15 seconds. Strain into a chilled coupe. Garnish with a lime wheel if you like.

SIMPLE SYRUP

Makes about 1½ cups

1 cup **granulated sugar**

8 ounces / 1 cup **filtered water**

In a small saucepan, combine the sugar and water. Cook over medium heat, stirring occasionally, until the sugar has dissolved, about 3 minutes. Remove the pan from the heat. Allow the syrup to cool before using. Store the syrup in an airtight container in the refrigerator for up to 2 weeks or in the freezer for up to 6 months.

SUBJECT YOURSELF TO:

Old Fashioned

The Old Fashioned is another example of three- or four- ingredient drinks transcending the simplicity of their structure. This drink works because the heat from the whiskey is balanced by the sweetness of the syrup and by dilution from the correct amount of stirring and ice. The bitters do not make the drink all that bitter; rather, they're like salt—adding it to the food you're cooking does not mean your dish will be salty, but you'll miss it if it's not there. Similarly, the bitters provide a structural backbone, giving the drink a little bit of bite to sustain the other flavors while adding a hint of aromatic complexity. Without the bitters, you're just drinking sweet cold whiskey in a glass, which isn't gross, but it's not really what cocktails are all about.

Expressing citrus oils over the top is important because doing so creates a sequence to drinking the drink. You first smell bright, fruity citrus notes as you get close, and then when you take a sip, the sensation transitions to the intense, spicy aromatics of the whiskey and bitters. People sometimes garnish an Old Fashioned with a cherry and/or an orange wedge, which I don't consider to be wrong—I will happily drink an Old Fashioned made this way—but I vastly prefer a peel with its oils expressed over the drink's surface because it's a more complex experience.

Since the overall volume of the mixed ingredients is just over 2 ounces, there is very little room to hide flaws here. Most people fuck this drink up by making it either too strong or not strong enough, or get scared and leave out the bitters. Don't do any of these things.

The Old Fashioned is a drink where having really nice big ice cubes can make a huge difference. Big ice is nice to have in finished cocktails served on the rocks because the cubes melt slowly, allowing you to sip at your leisure without the drink getting warm and watery before you're done. Big ice cubes also look really nice. The Old Fashioned in particular is characterized by its strength, and it can lose that strength if you're using tiny little bits of ice. So unless you're taking your Old Fashioned down all at once like a shot,* it's worth the effort to serve the drink with a big, clear chunk of ice.

Stirred drinks like this one need to be stirred. I know this sounds obvious, but I've seen people shake their stirred drinks countless times. Stirring retains the smooth texture of the ingredients by not incorporating air bubbles. It also allows you to dilute the drink enough to make it taste good, but not so much as to weaken the heat from the whiskey. Furthermore, cold temperatures shut down aromatics (think about cold coffee versus hot), so if you're drinking a too-cold Old Fashioned, you'll miss out on the delightful aromatic balance between the whiskey and the bitters.

Try swapping out the sweetener for honey or maple syrup, and experiment with infusing tea into the base spirit. You can also play with other types of bitters. Non-whiskey spirits such as rum, Cognac, and even gin can make unexpectedly tasty Old Fashioneds.

Makes 1 drink

2 ounces **rye or bourbon**

¼ ounce **Demerara Syrup** (recipe follows)

2 dashes **Angostura bitters**

1 dash **orange bitters** (optional)

Garnish Orange peel or lemon peel

In a mixing glass or shaking tin, combine the drink ingredients. Add ice and stir for 20 seconds. Strain into an old fashioned glass filled with one large ice cube. Garnish with a lemon or orange peel, expressed and then perched on the rim.

DEMERARA SYRUP

Makes about ¾ cup

1 cup **demerara sugar**

4 ounces / ½ cup **filtered water**

In a small saucepan, combine the sugar and water. Cook over medium heat, stirring occasionally, until the sugar has dissolved, about 3 minutes. Remove the pan from the heat. Allow the sugar to cool before using. Store the syrup in an airtight container in the refrigerator for up to 2 weeks or in the freezer for up to 6 months.

---

* This isn't the worst way to drink this drink but probably not the healthiest, either. . . .

SUBJECT YOURSELF TO:

Manhattan

This drink follows the pattern of two parts base spirit to one part vermouth plus bitters, a structure that pops up a lot. The vermouth, with its lower ABV—usually around 20%—balances out the heat from the whiskey while also providing its own complex set of aromatics, sweetness, and acidity, resulting in a relatively bright drink.

Manhattans are commonly flawed when people omit the bitters, don't use enough vermouth, or over-dilute by shaking. But this drink has some more places to hide flaws, so they may be harder to detect. For instance, sweet vermouth has a degree of bitterness but not enough to balance the drink on its own, so while the drink isn't garbage without the bitters, it's also not living its best life.

The most important balance point here is between the whiskey and the vermouth. Using half the amount of vermouth as of whiskey gives you enough aromatics and sweetness without making the drink too weak or overpowering the aromatics of the whiskey. With bitters, you want to use an amount that will enhance the flavor of the drink—the Angostura will give warm, spicy notes harmonious with those found in the whiskey and vermouth—but that won't crowd out the other ingredients. Leaving out the bitters here really shouldn't be an option.*

The Manhattan must be stirred with plenty of ice for fifteen to twenty seconds to become cold and diluted enough to be enjoyable, but not overly diluted so as to make the drink limp and flavorless. Some people like to

---

* Confession: I used to be one of those asshole bartenders who would openly judge and correct guests when they ordered drinks in a way I considered wrong. I would literally refuse to call a bitters-less Manhattan by its name. I'd tell people they'd ordered a "rye and vermouth." I'm nicer now, but I will still judge you if you leave out the bitters.

garnish their Manhattans with an orange peel, which I find to be a bit much, considering the aromatic complexity that already exists in the drink. Two delicious Luxardo cherries on a toothpick are a nice visual accompaniment to the drink, and they impart some of their tasty liquid while also soaking up the other ingredients. Eaten right after the last sip, they are a lovely coda to the experience.

The Manhattan is super riff-able (one of the best riffs out there is the Vieux Carré), but you don't have to get fancy. Swap out the rye with Scotch and it's a Rob Roy; make it with Cognac and it's a Harvard; Irish whiskey, an Emerald. Keep the vermouth and bitters and leave the measurements the same and you can also make this drink with rum, aged tequila, Japanese whisky . . . you get the idea. You can also play around with the vermouth, swapping out some or all of the sweet stuff for dry, or using sherry or Madeira if that's what you have available. And you can work with alternative bitters or with infusing the base spirit with things like tea or spices.

Makes 1 drink

2 ounces **rye or bourbon**

1 ounce **sweet vermouth**

2 dashes **Angostura bitters**

1 dash **orange bitters**

Garnish Luxardo cherries

In a mixing glass or shaking tin, combine the drink ingredients. Add ice and stir for 20 seconds. Strain into a chilled coupe. Garnish with Luxardo cherries speared on a toothpick.

SUBJECT YOURSELF TO:

Martini

The martini is structurally identical to the Manhattan, but flavor-wise the drinks are anything but alike. People also tend to have more feelings about the appropriate amount of vermouth used in a martini, so it's useful to consider the martini and Manhattan as distinct drinks.

My recipe might contain more vermouth than you're used to seeing in a martini, but I have very strong feelings about it. These strong feelings stem from the fact that this drink works for the same reasons the Manhattan does: there is enough vermouth to balance the base spirit. A martini isn't just a glass of chilled gin; a martini is a bright, herbal blend of gin, dry vermouth, and orange bitters, capped with an aromatic hit of lemon oil.

People love to ask for their martinis "dry," and I suspect this is the case for two reasons. One, because in this context, "dry" means the opposite of sweet—people love to think they don't like sweet things, even though they actually do. And two, because people wrongly believe the deeply harmful myth that vermouth is somehow gross. Vermouth is fucking delicious. I will guarantee you that most if not all of the people who think vermouth is gross have never actually tasted good fresh vermouth. In my years of bartending, unless someone specified that they wanted it dirty, no matter what they specified in terms of "dry," I would literally make them the drink according to this recipe.* None of them were ever sent back.

I would be remiss if I did not mention the unfortunate phenomenon of a shaken martini. I blame the James Bond franchise for this—people just hear some cool, attractive dude order something "shaken, not stirred" and want

---

* Unless they asked for no vermouth at all, in which case they just wanted chilled gin or vodka in a glass, which is a legitimate beverage choice but not really a cocktail as far as we're concerned.

in. In addition to introducing over-dilution and over-chilling, shaking breaks the ice into small chunks, and those chunks can end up your drink. Not many people want a martini with ice chips in it.*

While I seem pretty strict about the definition and recipe for a martini, there are a few ways to riff on it that rely solely on dialing up or down the amount of vermouth and gin. Yes, you can make a martini with a 7:1 ratio of gin to vermouth, or a 1:1 ratio, or even a 1:2 ratio. These are all valid and tasty, depending on your palate and where you like your balance to be. But if you think you like your martini with no vermouth and you've never tried it any other way, you owe it to yourself to try it the way I'm suggesting and take things from there.

The vodka martini is an example of a riff that has outshined the original in popularity, and so is the *dirty* martini, made with the inclusion of ¼ to ½ ounce of olive brine. The dirty martini is a great introduction to savory cocktails, illustrating that you can totally transform a cocktail with the small addition of an intensely flavored ingredient. As for other ways to riff on a martini aside from playing with proportions, you can play around a lot with the vermouth, replacing it with Lillet blanc, white vermouth, and even a light Fino or Manzanilla sherry, which are all structurally similar. Or you can replace the vermouth with sake and you'll have an honest-to-god saketini that you won't hate yourself for drinking, although you might still hate yourself for altogether different and valid reasons.

Makes 1 drink

2 ounces **gin**

1 ounce **dry vermouth**

3 dashes **orange bitters**

Garnish Lemon peel

In a mixing glass or shaking tin, combine the drink ingredients. Add ice and stir for 20 seconds. Strain into a chilled coupe. Garnish with a lemon peel, expressed and then perched on the rim.

---

* Some people do, though! And that's okay, but not most people.

SUBJECT YOURSELF TO:

Margarita

This drink is similar to the daiquiri, but the sweetener has been replaced with orange liqueur. My favorite liqueur in a margarita is Cointreau. Alternatively, Grand Marnier is slightly richer, or go for blue curaçao if you're a cool person and love life and joy. Any of these have a fair amount of sweetness as well as 20% ABV or more. This means that the alcohol balance point of a margarita is higher than that of a daiquiri—it's a stronger drink. I do still include ¼ ounce of agave syrup to give the drink a fuller body and to balance out the acidity from the lime juice and orange liqueur. Most orange liqueurs have a bit of bitterness to them—they are flavored with the skins of bitter oranges—so yes, a margarita should be a tiny bit bitter. It provides a nice backbone for the rest of the flavors, making this drink slightly more complex than a simple daiquiri. Many people salt the rims of their margaritas, which helps to balance out a bit of the bitterness from the orange liqueur as well as amplify some of the briny notes from the tequila. Also, salt just makes things taste better.

Aromatically, this drink is all about the interplay between the green, fruity, vegetal (and sometimes floral and mineral) notes from the tequila and the citrus notes from the orange liqueur and lime juice. The agave syrup offers a bit of an earthy, almost maple syrup-like aroma, which makes it a superior choice to simple syrup, but your margarita will be just fine if you don't have access to agave nectar or you don't feel like using it for whatever reason.

The biggest margarita-related crime is using bad tequila. Many people hate tequila because they overdid it on bad tequila shots in high school[*] and never experienced the good stuff. Kind of like if you thought all cheese was Kraft Singles and Polly-O string cheese and never tasted a decent Gruyère or mozzarella.

---

[*]   Middle school?

Some people like their margaritas on the rocks, either because they nurse them slowly or because they simply like the experience of having ice in the glass and the little extra dilution it offers. It's a personal choice.

You can find a tremendous variation in margaritas simply by switching the kind of tequila and orange liqueur you use. Try one with blanco and Cointreau, and try another with reposado and Grand Marnier, or swap the tequila for mezcal. This drink can take many forms, including a slushy frozen variety, but you won't find a recipe for that here.

The margarita, and its fraternal twin, the sidecar, belong to a category of drinks I call Daisies. This category—with 1¾ ounces base, ¾ ounce citrus, ¾ ounce liqueur, and ¼ ounce sweetener—is so named because *margarita* means "daisy" in Spanish. You can use the Daisy template to rifle through a ton of spirits and fruit liqueurs to create an innumerable variety of cocktails.

Makes 1 drink

1¾ ounces **tequila**

¾ ounce **orange liqueur, such as Cointreau**

¾ ounce **fresh lime juice**

¼ ounce **Agave Syrup** (recipe follows)

Optional Garnishes Salt and/or lime wheel

In a shaker, combine the drink ingredients. Add ice and shake for 15 seconds. Strain into a chilled coupe or an ice-filled rocks glass. If you want to salt the rim of the glass, use a piece of cut lime to wet the rim of the glass, and then dip the rim in the salt to coat it.* Garnish with a lime wheel if you like.

AGAVE SYRUP
Makes about 1 cup

6 ounces / ¾ cup **agave nectar**

6 ounces / ¾ cup **filtered water**

In a small bowl, whisk together the agave nectar and water. Store the syrup in an airtight container in the refrigerator for up to 2 weeks or in the freezer for up to 6 months.

* Just make sure you do this before you pour the drink, because it's very awkward/impossible to do it once the drink is in the glass.

SUBJECT YOURSELF TO:

Cosmopolitan
Fun and tart
PAGE 105

Sidecar
Rich and fruity
PAGE 108

Johnny's Margarita
Herbaceous and vegetal
PAGE 114

Baroque Daisy
Ornate and challenging
PAGE 147

Melted Firecracker Margarita
Silly and sweet
PAGE 185

Flower Powers
Spirit-forward and floral
PAGE 202

Highball

A Highball is not just a whiskey and soda. A whiskey and soda represents a resignation to sloppiness—a free pour of cheap whiskey and a careless splash of limp soda—whereas a Highball draws from a long-standing Japanese tradition of precision. If you go to a fancy cocktail bar in Japan, chances are you'll see a be-suited bartender spend five to ten minutes executing an elaborate ritual to make this drink. It's both fascinating and infuriating to watch.*

The Highball works primarily because it's so fucking simple. This drink's goal is to bring whiskey down to a beer-like strength so that you can enjoy it in a similar manner and quantity, usually alongside food. Following this recipe, the resulting Highball clocks in at about 10% ABV, with the point being to render the beverage more quaffable while still retaining the aromatics of the whiskey. In fact, some aromatics become more present and noticeable once you've moved the alcohol out of the way, giving your palate a chance to pick up on subtleties you would otherwise be distracted from noticing.

Consider the 3:1 ratio you see here as a starting point. If you find you prefer something weaker or stronger, great. And you can decide which whiskies work best with each dilution level—a milder Japanese whisky works nicely at 3:1, while a hotter, spicier rye might be more enjoyable at 4:1. Play around.

To produce this drink exactly right, you really need to focus on the carbonation. The delicate bubbles you get from a bottle of sparkling mineral water are far different from the bigger, more forceful ones in canned seltzer or from a countertop carbonation unit. Find what you like best.

---

* Fortunately, you can also buy canned Highballs in Japanese convenience stores (*konbini*), which is almost enough for me to pack up and permanently relocate there.

Carbonation is also something you need to work to maintain, because carbon dioxide quickly dissipates from water. Gas dissolves more readily at cold temperatures, so keeping the water as cold as possible will help you maintain the bubbles until the drink gets to your mouth. It's also not a bad idea to chill the whiskey itself before mixing.

One of the most successful Highball riffs—one so successful that it eclipses the Highball's popularity by many orders of magnitude—is the gin and tonic. Hell, people have written whole-ass books on the thing. I could have written about the gin and tonic separately, but if you really look at the structure of the cocktail, it's a Highball, or a Highball is a gin and tonic. They are secretly more alike than they are different, because when you boil it down, you're still working with three parts bubbles to one part spirit.

Some other fun riffs on the Highball include using literally any spirit you have on hand, making this a great in-a-pinch cocktail. You can also play around with flavored bubbly waters like La Croix. Notable riffs include rum and Coke, whiskey and ginger ale, vodka soda (duh), and rye and Dr Pepper. Try making one with an amaro like Campari for an excellent introduction to the complex and intense world of bitter liqueurs.

Makes 1 drink

6 ounces / ¾ cup **chilled sparkling water**

1½ ounces **whiskey, preferably Japanese or Scotch**

Optional Garnishes Fresh mint leaf or a citrus wedge

Pour 2 ounces of the sparkling water into a tall ice-filled glass. Add the whiskey. Add the remaining 4 ounces sparkling water. If you like, garnish with a mint leaf or citrus wedge of your choice. Serve with a straw if desired.

The technique to maintain maximum carbonation is something I like to call the Soda Sandwich. You'll notice that this recipe calls for an amount of soda (sparkling water) to be placed in the glass first, with the whiskey added next, and then more sparkling water poured on top. This sandwiching of ingredients allows them to mix without necessitating further agitation, which can reduce the bubbles, and the bubbles are the whole point of this drink.

SUBJECT YOURSELF TO:

Tom Collins

The Tom Collins is a deliberately over-diluted drink. This drink is very forgiving because the sparkling water acts as a lengthener; a lengthened drink's larger overall volume tends to smooth out any rough edges. The botanicals from the gin should be gentle but perceptible—you want to know they're there, but you don't want the gin to kick you in the kneecaps and steal your wallet.

The dry shake is an essential technique here because the drink depends on the right amount of dilution from the sparkling water and not from the still water that would melt off the ice during standard shaking. A dry shake mixes and froths the cocktail before you introduce it to the sparkling water and ice in the glass. Many bartenders shake a Tom Collins with ice—the rationale being that you're trading some extra dilution in exchange for chilling the mixed ingredients—but I'd rather not make this trade-off. If extreme coldness is important to you, I'd rather see you pre-chill all the ingredients.

Playing around with base spirits is a great way to riff, as is subbing out unflavored bubbly for something flavored. You can even ditch water altogether and replace it with sparkling wine or beer. Tinker with the citrus, with flavored syrups, and with spirit infusions as well.

Makes 1 drink

2 ounces **gin**

¾ ounce **fresh lemon juice**

¾ ounce **Simple Syrup**
(page 68)

4 to 6 ounces / ½ to ¾ cup
chilled sparkling water

Optional Garnish Lemon wheel

In a shaker, combine the gin, lemon juice, and simple syrup. Dry shake for 5 seconds. Pour 2 ounces of the sparkling water into a tall ice-filled Collins or water glass, and empty the contents of the shaker into the prepared glass. Top up with the remaining 2 to 4 ounces sparkling water. Garnish with a lemon wheel and serve with a straw if you like.

SUBJECT YOURSELF TO:

El Diablo

Spicy and fruity

PAGE 106

Saffron Collins

Elegant and herbal

PAGE 141

Pineapple Scotch Punch

Fruity and festive

PAGE 157

Watermelon Fennel Collins

Refreshing and sober

PAGE 178

Whiskey Sour

This drink shows how adding a single ingredient—here, an egg white—can completely transform a cocktail. When you shake a drink with egg white, you first shake with no ice to whip the white. On a molecular level, you are straightening out the proteins in the egg white. These longer, straighter proteins are more likely to stack up and create matrices for air bubbles to get trapped in, which is why egg white drinks have such a great frothy texture. Cold temperatures slow this process, hence the first dry shake to unfold the proteins and then a second with ice to chill, dilute, and further aerate.

I've found that egg white has a slightly tannic, grippy, almost astringent texture that is balanced out by the addition of a whole ounce of simple syrup. Some people also like to up the citrus here to 1 ounce—it just depends how strong you want your drink to be. I want this drink to taste like whiskey, which is why I use only ¾ ounce. You want it to be tart—think about lemon meringue pie—but you're not quite at the sharpness you find in a daiquiri. The bitters are an aromatic mask for the sometimes-earthy/barnyard-y scent of the raw egg; they're not really making the drink that bitter.

There are a lot of ways to fuck up this drink, though. It should go without saying that you should never use sour mix, but I *am* saying it here just in case. Other common problems: not enough sweetener (the tannins from the egg white overpower); too much sweetener (cloying); and bad whiskey (bad). That said, try to find a whiskey that is good enough, but not so good that it would be overkill.

Try out different base spirits. A rye whiskey sour will be very different from one made with bourbon, but you can also try it with Scotch, Japanese, and Irish whiskies. An absinthe rinse is a simple but powerful augmentation.

Makes 1 drink

2 ounces **whiskey, preferably bourbon**

1 ounce **Simple Syrup** (page 68)

¾ ounce **fresh lemon juice**

1 **egg white**

Optional Garnishes Bitters, such as Angostura, and/or Luxardo cherries

In a shaker, combine the drink ingredients. Dry shake for 5 seconds. Add ice and shake for an additional 15 seconds. Strain into a chilled coupe or old fashioned glass. Garnish with a few dashes of bitters over the top if desired. Add Luxardo cherries, speared on a pick, if you like.

SUBJECT YOURSELF TO:

Pisco Sour

Fruity and fun

PAGE 111

Amaretto Sour / Midori Sour

Tacky but secretly amazing

PAGE 126

White Birch Fizz

Elegant and herbal

PAGE 135

Last Word

I love this drink. But I would actually never drink one because I cannot stand the taste of green Chartreuse—kind of like how certain people can't handle cilantro. I recognize that green Chartreuse is a very well made product with a lot of interesting history and aromatic complexity, but there is a barnyard/hay note that I just can't get past. The reason I love this drink is completely academic: it works in spite of its odd structure, and in spite of the fact that it has so many intensely flavored elements, which somehow come together harmoniously to create an emergent and distinct flavor.

If you squint, you can see how this drink is a simple sour, whereby the Chartreuse and Maraschino liqueurs serve double duty as both a base spirit and a sweetener. There is enough alcohol in this drink to make it taste strong, and there is enough sweetness in this drink to make it palatable and give it body, with the lime juice providing the acidity to balance out the heavy sweetness of the Chartreuse and Maraschino. The Chartreuse offers just a bit of bitterness, giving that backbone to bind the flavors together.

As with other shaken drinks, it's vulnerable to the same flaws: not shaken enough or served with not enough ice. Unlike some more-forgiving drinks, this one can really get thrown off if you're not careful when measuring, since each ingredient is such a heavyweight.

I also love this drink because you can go wild riffing it. I classify drinks that follow this four-equal-part structure as Quartets. Simple riffs on the Last Word replace the gin with tequila, mezcal, or white rum. If you want to slide into brown spirits, you should, but you'll find the drink probably tastes better with lemon juice and yellow Chartreuse instead of green, which can be overpowering.

Makes 1 drink

¾ ounce **gin**

¾ ounce **green Chartreuse**

¾ ounce **Luxardo Maraschino liqueur**

¾ ounce **fresh lime juice**

In a shaker, combine the drink ingredients. Add ice and shake vigorously for 15 seconds. Strain into a chilled coupe.

SUBJECT YOURSELF TO:

Corpse Reviver
Number Blue

Blue and delicious

Weed Punch

Herbal and intense

The Summer Quartet

Challenging and complex

FEELING CLASSIC

These drinks are either classic cocktails or rely heavily on classic cocktail structure. The recipes here are probably the most broadly applicable to a wide variety of situations and preferences. Classics are different from the archetypes of the previous section in that they represent specific recipes, rather than templates on which to build and riff.

Cosmopolitan

The cosmopolitan is a fantastic cocktail and deserves a place among the Great Classics. Most people who dislike this drink either haven't had a properly made one, dislike pink drinks in general, or have a negative association with the women of *Sex and the City*. These are all silly reasons for disliking an excellent drink.

You'll notice that structurally the cosmopolitan is a lot like the sidecar (and the margarita). It's another example of a basic sour modified with a liqueur, so the base spirit and other sweeteners must be brought back in a bit in order to maintain the drink's balance.

Makes 1 drink

1¾ ounces **citron vodka** (I like Hangar One's Buddha's Hand)

¾ ounce **fresh lemon juice**

¾ ounce **Cointreau**

¼ ounce **cranberry juice** (see page 44)

Garnish Lime wheel

In a shaker, combine the drink ingredients. Add ice and shake for 15 seconds. Strain into a chilled coupe and garnish with a lime wheel.

El Diablo

There are a ton of different ways to make an El Diablo. I'm sure there is a definitive version somewhere out there, but that's an unimportant endeavor next to finding a recipe you actually like. To start, here's a version that I love. Most people use ginger beer, but I think it's 1000% better with sparkling wine. This drink is a bit bigger in volume than usual, which is why I recommend serving it with ice in an old fashioned or water glass. The ice helps soften the intensity from the ginger and provides additional dilution to balance the alcohol.

Makes 1 drink

1½ ounces **reposado tequila**

¾ ounce **Ginger Syrup** (recipe follows)

¾ ounce **fresh lime juice**

¾ ounce **Lejay crème de cassis**

2 ounces **sparkling wine, such as Cava or Prosecco**

Garnishes Lime wheel and candied ginger on a pick

In a shaker, combine the tequila, ginger syrup, lime juice, and crème de cassis. Add ice and shake for 15 seconds. Strain into an ice-filled old fashioned or water glass. Top with the sparkling wine and garnish with the lime wheel and candied ginger.

GINGER SYRUP
Makes about 2 cups

2 pounds **fresh ginger,** thoroughly scrubbed*

About 2 cups **granulated sugar** (depending on juice yield; see Note)

Using a juice extractor, juice the ginger. Pass the liquid through a gold coffee filter to remove all solids. You should have about 1 cup. Combine the ginger juice and sugar in a small saucepan. Cook, stirring occasionally, over medium heat until all the sugar has dissolved. Remove the pan from the heat and allow the syrup to cool for a few minutes. Place the pan in an ice bath and stir every few minutes until the mixture is below room temperature. Use immediately or store in an airtight container in the refrigerator for up to 2 weeks or in the freezer for up to 6 months.

---

* I prefer the more robust flavor of unpeeled ginger, but you can peel it if you think doing so is worth your time.

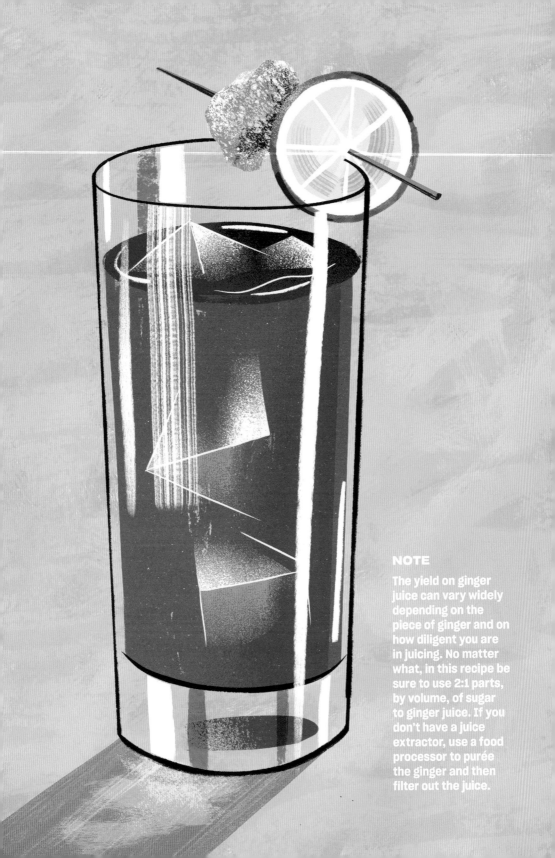

NOTE

The yield on ginger juice can vary widely depending on the piece of ginger and on how diligent you are in juicing. No matter what, in this recipe be sure to use 2:1 parts, by volume, of sugar to ginger juice. If you don't have a juice extractor, use a food processor to purée the ginger and then filter out the juice.

Sidecar

There are a lot of different sidecar recipes floating around, but this version is my favorite. You'll notice that the structure is exactly the same as that of the Margarita on page 83. The sidecar is a very straightforward and ubiquitous cocktail, but one I suspect not many people have actually tried.

Feel free to use any Cognac you like—VS or VSOP—or you can even try Calvados, a French apple brandy. Just keep in mind that the presence of the lemon juice and orange liqueur can overshadow more expensive brandies, so there's no need to spend a fortune. My go-to orange liqueur for sidecars is Cointreau, thanks to its bright flavor and tiny bit of bitterness. If you don't have Cointreau on hand, feel free to sub it out for any orange liqueur—you won't need to adjust the proportions. Some people feel the need to rim the glass with sugar. I am not one of those people, so I will not give you instructions for it.

Makes 1 drink

1¾ ounces **Cognac**
¾ ounce **fresh lemon juice**
¾ ounce **Cointreau**
¼ ounce **Simple Syrup**
　(page 68)

In a shaker, combine the drink ingredients. Add ice and shake for 15 seconds. Strain into a chilled coupe.

Sazerac

This drink is basically an Old Fashioned (page 71) with an absinthe rinse and without ice.

For a long time I thought the original, authentic Sazerac was made with Cognac instead of rye. Apparently, that's not true. Ultimately, I'm more concerned with making drinks that I like than I am with authenticity—and that's my goal for you, too. In my years of making, serving, and drinking Sazeracs, I've found that the most delicious version is made with a split base of Cognac and rye. This mix provides a little more interest and complexity.

Serving a Sazerac in an old fashioned glass with no ice serves a purpose similar to serving red wine in a large-bowl wine glass: the glass best captures the layered aromatics from the absinthe, whiskey, bitters, and lemon oil.

Makes 1 drink

Absinthe, for rinsing

1 ounce **rye**

1 ounce **Cognac**

¼ ounce **Demerara Syrup** (page 72)

3 dashes **Peychaud's bitters**

2 dashes **Angostura bitters**

Lemon peel

Rinse a chilled old fashioned glass with absinthe. In a mixing glass or shaking tin, combine the rye, Cognac, demerara syrup, and both bitters. Add ice and stir for 20 seconds. Strain into the prepared glass. Express the lemon peel over the top, then discard the peel before serving.

NOTE Splitting the base of a cocktail is an easy, high-value tweak to jazz up the drink, and I encourage you to try it out for other drinks as well.

Pisco Sour

The structure here is almost identical to that of the Whiskey Sour on page 95. There are a lot of uninspiring pisco sours out there. Many are too sweet, and others suffer from hastily shaken egg whites, which causes an unappealing texture.

This is a fun drink to play around with basic riffs, like swapping the base spirit, substituting honey for the simple syrup, or changing up the bitters. Just don't skip the bitters, as they provide a nice aromatic cap to the drink and, especially, help cover up any eggy aroma from the egg white. You can add the bitters drop by drop or spray them in a mist.

Makes 1 drink

2 ounces **pisco, such as Macchu Pisco**

½ ounce **fresh lemon juice**

½ ounce **fresh lime juice**

¾ ounce **Simple Syrup** (page 68)

1 **egg white**

Garnish Angostura bitters

In a shaker, combine the drink ingredients. Dry shake for 3 seconds. Add ice and shake again for 15 seconds. Strain into a chilled coupe. Garnish with 4 or 5 drops of Angostura bitters across the top.

NOTE Sometimes egg white drinks can be kind of heavy, so I use an ounce of citrus in lighter egg white drinks like this one.

Mountainside

Initially, back when it was available and relatively cheap, I made this drink with Yamazaki twelve-year Japanese whisky. Now, thanks to the surge in demand for Japanese whisky, Yamazaki twelve-year is a bit too expensive to go throwing into a cocktail. Fortunately, Suntory, the producer of Yamazaki twelve-year, has released two younger whiskies that are great in this drink: Toki and Hibiki. This would also work nicely with Irish whiskey in a pinch.

This drink is an Old Fashioned through and through. The only change is that the sugar syrup here is flavored. I pick up a slight hint of fennel in Suntory's whiskies, so I matched it with a fennel syrup to bring that observation to the forefront of the drinking experience.

Makes 1 drink

2 ounces **Japanese whisky**

¼ ounce **Fennel Syrup** (recipe follows)

3 dashes **orange bitters**

Garnish Grapefruit peel

In a mixing glass or shaking tin, combine the drink ingredients. Add ice and stir for 15 seconds. Strain into a chilled rocks glass filled with ice. Garnish with a grapefruit peel, expressed and then perched on the rim.

FENNEL SYRUP
Makes about 1 cup

8 ounces / 1 cup **Simple Syrup** (page 68)

30 grams **fennel seeds**

In a blender, combine the simple syrup with the fennel seeds and blend on high speed for 3 minutes, until the fennel seeds are completely demolished. Strain through a gold coffee filter, discarding any solids. Store in an airtight container in the refrigerator for up to 2 weeks or in the freezer for up to 6 months.

NOTE Matching flavors from spirits with other ingredients is an excellent tool to help decide what flavors to put together when creating your own drinks.

Johnny's Margarita

This drink was the first I created at Momofuku Ssäm Bar. It's not a classic cocktail in the formal sense, but it is based on one: the Tommy's Margarita. Tommy's Margarita is a stripped-down margarita—it has no orange liqueur. This is essentially a Tommy's Margarita, but with a spray of absinthe over the top. I serve it in an old fashioned glass without ice, which provides a more impactful aromatic experience. When someone goes to drink it, they're first hit with the fennel, anise, and licorice from the absinthe, and once they take a sip, those aromas are contrasted with the bright flavors of lime and tequila. It's a great introduction to absinthe.

And for the record, no, I did not name this drink after myself. I am very vain and narcissistic but I'm not *that* bad. When I was presenting the drink to the staff and explaining that it was based on a Tommy's Margarita, one of my managers at the time blurted out "Johnny's Margarita!!" in front of the whole staff, and it stuck. So I guess he named it after me.

Makes 1 drink

2 ounces **blanco tequila**

¾ ounce **fresh lime juice**

¾ ounce **Agave Syrup** (page 84)

Absinthe, in a spray bottle, for finishing

In a shaker, combine the tequila, lime juice, and agave syrup. Add ice and shake for 15 seconds. Strain into a chilled old fashioned glass. Spray a mist of absinthe over the top before serving.

Negroni / Boulevardier / Old Pal

I am lumping these three drinks together to show that you can get a lot of mileage out of simple ingredient swaps, which allow you to be creative quite easily and also enable you to make drinks in a pinch when you're missing an ingredient and need a backup plan.

The Negroni is an excellent drink that's been having an ongoing moment, but its cousins, the Boulevardier and the Old Pal, do not always get the same level of attention. All three are equally delicious, and all happen to be quite food friendly,* so keep that in mind for your next dinner party.

I prefer a London dry-style gin with my Negroni—something with a really strong juniper presence—but feel free to play around with others if you like. I go with bourbon in my Boulevardier and rye in my Old Pal.

Each recipe makes 1 drink

Negroni

1 ounce **London dry gin**

1 ounce **Campari**

1 ounce **Italian sweet vermouth**

Garnish Orange wedge

Boulevardier

1 ounce **bourbon**

1 ounce **Campari**

1 ounce **Italian sweet vermouth**

Garnish Orange peel

Old Pal

1 ounce **rye**

1 ounce **Campari**

1 ounce **dry vermouth**

Garnish Lemon peel

In a mixing glass or shaking tin, combine the drink ingredients. Add ice and stir for 15 seconds. Strain into a rocks glass filled with ice. Garnish with an orange wedge for a Negroni; for a Boulevardier, express an orange peel and then perch it on the rim; express a lemon peel and perch it on the rim for an Old Pal.

---

* Meaning they go well with food.

Corpse Reviver Number Blue

I'm a blue drinks guy. Ever since I put The Shark (page 155) on the menu at PDT in 2013, I've had a bit of a reputation as someone who helped make blue drinks acceptable to the snooty craft cocktail scene. Pioneered by blue-drinks evangelist Jacob Briars, the Corpse Reviver Number Blue is a take on the classic Corpse Reviver Number Two, but with a simple substitution of blue curaçao for regular orange curaçao or Triple Sec. If you were blindfolded, this drink would taste exactly the same, but here, the addition of blue coloring has a significant impact on the overall sensory experience. It's fun to drink an electric blue drink every once and a while.

I specifically like Plymouth gin here because it has a soft juniper profile that doesn't overpower everything else, but you can use whatever you have on hand. Lillet blanc is a French aromatized wine somewhat similar to dry vermouth.

Makes 1 drink

Absinthe, for rinsing
¾ ounce **Plymouth gin**
¾ ounce **Lillet blanc**
¾ ounce **blue curaçao**
¾ ounce **fresh lemon juice**

Rinse a chilled coupe with absinthe. In a shaker, combine all the remaining ingredients. Add ice and shake for 15 seconds. Strain into the prepared coupe.

NOTE Once you open the bottle of Lillet, keep it in the fridge and be sure to drink it within a few weeks. If it gets any older than that, it won't be undrinkable, but it won't be awesome.

Vieux Carré

This drink is one of my all-time favorites. It's got a ton of complexity, and the structure of the recipe is ripe for exploring riffs. It's kind of a mash-up of a Manhattan, with its two parts of base to one of vermouth, and an Old Fashioned, with the inclusion of an added sweetener, Bénédictine. Bénédictine is a French herbal liqueur containing hyssop, myrrh, aloe, thyme, coriander, vanilla, cinnamon, and nutmeg. Officially there is no garnish for this drink, but sometimes I like to throw a few Luxardo cherries in just for fun.

The Vieux Carré is a perfect example of how a cocktail can tell a story. By most credible accounts, this drink was created at the Hotel Monteleone in New Orleans's French Quarter. *Vieux Carré* is French for "old square," which is a reference to the quarter. Like the city itself, this drink is a fusion of French, American, and Caribbean influences, reflected in the French Cognac, vermouth, and Bénédictine; American rye whiskey; and Angostura from Trinidad. And lastly, the Peychaud's is a New Orleans native.

Makes 1 drink

1 ounce **rye**

1 ounce **Cognac**

1 ounce **Dolin Rouge vermouth**

⅛ ounce **Bénédictine**

3 dashes **Peychaud's bitters**

2 dashes **Angostura bitters**

Optional Garnish Luxardo cherries

In a mixing glass or shaking tin, combine the drink ingredients. Add ice and stir for 20 seconds. Strain into an ice-filled old fashioned glass. Garnish with Luxardo cherries if you like.

FEELING LAZY

Laziness is a virtue. Not to be confused with sloth, laziness is simply the desire to avoid unnecessary work. With that in mind, these recipes are easy and involve high-value, low-work steps. Some allow you to do more with less, and some front-load the work—having you prepare batches in advance, for instance—as a gift to your future self. That said, these drinks still abide by the rules of objective deliciousness, but with ingredients and preparation techniques to suit your lazy ass.

Death in the Afternoon

Apparently this was one of Ernest Hemingway's favorite drinks, or maybe he even created it. Whatever. Who cares. What's important is that this drink provides an opportunity to talk about how everyone loves a good D in the A. It's a high-proof mixture of wine and absinthe, so a D in the A can be intense at first; maybe it's something you need to work up to.

This drink represents, structurally, the bare minimum of what a cocktail is: two things mixed together. And yet, due to the underlying complexity of the absinthe, the resulting flavor is challenging and elevated. It demonstrates beautifully that you don't need to make big moves in order to make a big impact.

Champagne is preferred here, but you can use Cava or Prosecco if you like. And some people prefer to add ¼ ounce of simple syrup, or even throw some ice cubes in the drink. I won't stop you.

Makes 1 drink

5 ounces **chilled Champagne**

1 ounce **absinthe**

¼ ounce **Simple Syrup**
(optional; page 68)

Pour the Champagne into a wine glass, then drop the absinthe on top and give it a quick stir. Stir in the simple syrup if you like, and add ice if desired.

Preserves Sour

Fruit preserves are one of my favorite things to have around. They offer a consistent flavor and sweetness no matter the climate or season, and you can get them pretty much anywhere. Dropping a plop into your shaking tin is a great lazy way to spruce up an otherwise unremarkable cocktail—and you don't even have to bother making simple syrup to sweeten it.

Feel free to riff on this, based on your mood, preference, or whatever ingredients you have. Some suggestions: vodka and anything; gin and raspberry; tequila and fig; rye and cherry; pisco and strawberry; rum and plum; bourbon and orange marmalade. You can also play around with which citrus—lemon or lime—works best for each combination.

Makes 1 drink

2 ounces **Irish whiskey**
½ ounce **fresh lemon juice**
2 teaspoons **peach preserves**

In a shaking tin, combine the drink ingredients. Add ice and shake for 15 seconds. Fine-strain into a chilled cocktail glass.

Beached Mint-Lime Cooler

I'm a big fan of drinking at the beach, but it's not always easy to pull off. The local options are frequently overpriced—or nonexistent—and bringing your own supply risks your being faced with warm drinks by the time you actually settle in. The trick is to make this drink the night before and let it chill in the freezer overnight. That way it will be extremely, overly cold when you pull it out of the freezer, but if you time it just right, you'll have a perfectly chilled drink ready to go as soon as you arrive—1½ to 2 hours from your departure.* The water in the mixture makes up for the water you would otherwise get from shaking with ice. Obviously, this trick applies to many other outdoor locations or parties. This drink would also work nicely with other white spirits such as white rum or gin, even pisco or tequila.

Makes about 5 drinks

10 ounces / 1¼ cups **vodka**

4 ounces / ½ cup **fresh lime juice**

4 ounces / ½ cup **Mint Simple Syrup** (recipe follows)

8 ounces / 1 cup **filtered water**

Using a funnel if necessary, pour all the ingredients into a 1-liter bottle and give it a little shake. Place the bottle in the freezer to chill overnight.

MINT SIMPLE SYRUP
Makes about 1½ cups

8 ounces / 1 cup **filtered water**

1 cup **granulated sugar**

10 to 15 **fresh mint leaves**

In a blender, combine all the ingredients and blend on high speed for 2 minutes, until the sugar has dissolved. Strain through a gold coffee filter, discarding any solids. Store in an airtight container in the refrigerator for up to 2 weeks or in the freezer for up to 6 months.

---

* Just make sure the bottle you're using is at least 1 liter in capacity, to account for the expansion caused by freezing, and is not insulated. Insulated bottles will take forever to freeze and thaw.

Amaretto Sour / Midori Sour

Are you thinking that the only thing grosser than an Amaretto Sour is a Midori Sour? Not so! Just as you can have really good pizza and really shitty pizza, the fault is not in the idea of what a pizza is but rather in the execution. These drinks fail when people don't know how to use liqueurs properly and end up making something too sweet. The recipes here strip it down to the bare essentials, offering a tasty—and most important—easy, low-ABV cocktail.

I grouped these drinks together because, like the Negroni / Boulevardier / Old Pal (page 115), they are virtually the same drink, made different with simple ingredient swaps. This recipe will also work well for other liqueurs, such as raspberry liqueur and lime juice, and Frangelico and lemon juice.

Each recipe makes 1 drink

Amaretto Sour

2 ounces **Luxardo Amaretto liqueur**

1 ounce **fresh lemon juice**

1 **egg white**

Garnishes Luxardo cherries and bitters, such as Angostura (optional)

Midori Sour

2 ounces **Midori**

1 ounce **fresh lime juice**

1 **egg white**

Optional Garnish Lime wheel

In a shaker, combine the drink ingredients. Dry shake for 5 seconds. Add ice and shake again for 15 seconds. Strain into a chilled old fashioned glass filled with ice. For the Amaretto Sour, garnish with Luxardo cherries, and spray or dash some Angostura over the top if desired; for the Midori Sour you can perch a lime wheel on the rim if you're feeling fancy.

Meal-Prepper Martini

There is something classic about the idea of coming home to a well-made martini after a long day. The only problem is that most of us don't have someone waiting at home with a martini in hand, and rummaging through your empty apartment to make one for yourself is a little sad. What if we applied the same concept to cocktails as we do to meal prep. Meal prep exists in a world where people have the time and inclination to make a big batch of food on Sunday, and then have the discipline and a predictable-enough schedule to eat and enjoy those meals during the week. I can't imagine how boring you have to be in order for this to be a viable solution to life every single week. What I can imagine, though, is making a big batch of martinis so you have a few bottles full of them in the freezer, just waiting for you to pour into a chilled glass (although you might need to let it thaw out for a few minutes). This will stay tasty for much longer than two weeks in the freezer, but the flavor of the vermouth might start to fade a bit beyond two weeks.

Makes about 12 drinks (2 weeks' worth)

1 (750mL) bottle of **gin**
1 (375mL) bottle of **dry vermouth**
¼ ounce **orange bitters**
375mL **filtered water***

Pour all the ingredients into a large container, such as a deep mixing bowl or a 4-quart Cambro, and stir to combine. Using a funnel if necessary, re-bottle the mixture, leaving room for expansion due to freezing, in the gin and vermouth bottles, plus an extra bottle or airtight container for the excess. Freeze for up to 2 weeks.

NOTE This meal prep concept can also be applied to the Manhattan. Follow the same steps, but replace the gin with rye (or bourbon, if that's you), use sweet vermouth, and add ¼ ounce Angostura in addition to the orange bitters.

---

* Hot tip: Use the empty vermouth bottle to measure out the filtered water.

Getting Weird at the Beach

Like the Beached Mint-Lime Cooler on page 125, this is an easy drink you can throw into a water bottle the night before a trip to the beach, giving you a semi-slushy yet surprisingly sophisticated tropical treat that should stay cold for about three hours. The passion fruit, along with pineapple and grenadine, provides bright acidity. Drink this the next time you want to get weird at the beach.

Makes about 5 drinks

6 ounces / ¾ cup **white rum** (dark rum is okay, too)

4½ ounces **frozen passion fruit purée, such as Boiron, thawed**

4½ ounces **pineapple juice**

2¼ ounces **Grenadine** (recipe follows)

1½ ounces **absinthe**

3 ounces **filtered water**

Using a funnel if necessary, pour all the ingredients into a 1-liter (or larger) noninsulated bottle, give it a shake to combine, and store it in the freezer overnight. Remove the bottle from the freezer at least an hour before serving.

GRENADINE
Makes about 1 cup

8 ounces / 1 cup **100% pomegranate juice**

1 cup **granulated sugar**

In a blender, combine the juice and sugar and blend on high speed for about 1 minute, until the sugar has dissolved. Allow the air bubbles to settle before using it. Store in an airtight container in the refrigerator for up to 2 weeks or in the freezer for up to 6 months.

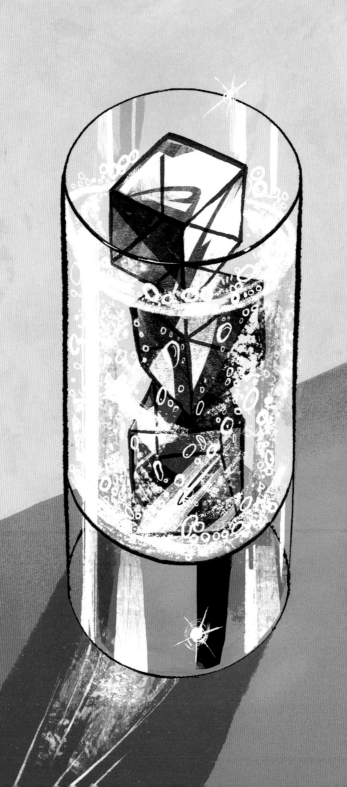

Lazy (Fancy) Vodka Soda

Have you ever had iced coffee where the ice was also coffee? If not, try it, then slide into those DMs to me to tell me how I changed your life. Then, imagine that magic in a cocktail. Making a vodka soda with non-water ice cubes is such a simple, but high-value, way to snazz up a vodka soda. That's not to imply that vodka soda drinkers are easily impressed, but it's not *not* to imply it either.

If you've followed my advice for making real cranberry juice on page 44, you'll likely already have a tray of cranberry juice cubes waiting for you in your freezer. You literally just make a vodka soda (a vodka Highball, essentially, see pages 87-88) and use the cranberry cubes instead of ice cubes. I'm not even giving you a fucking recipe for this because I'm allowed to be lazy, too.

FEELING FANCY

Sometimes you want to impress people, and for me, one of the best ways to do that is by showing that you have the time, dedication, and resources to devote to doing something really well. These drinks require a certain amount of work, or expense, or both. They are also a bit more intricate than others in this book, requiring attention to detail. Impressing people, including yourself, is a rewarding endeavor every once in a while. With these drinks you can do that and expand your capabilities—and as a bonus, you're left with a delicious* drink at the end of it.

* (hopefully)

White Birch Fizz

I invented this drink on White Birch Lane, where I grew up. It was one of the first drinks I ever created, back when I thought it was fun to bring a bunch of obscure bottles with me on the train to my parents' house and sling cocktails in their kitchen instead of just having a gin and tonic or a glass of wine like a normal person. My goal was to make a cocktail that would convince my wine-loving mother, Victoria—who was not sold on my new career trajectory—that cocktails were actually good.

So I made a variation on the Ramos Gin Fizz using Plymouth gin, apricot brandy—apricot being one of my mom's favorite flavors—and Strega, an Italian herbal liqueur similar to yellow Chartreuse, with a spray of Suze, a French gentian apéritif, over the top.

After the first round, we got to chatting about what to call it. My husband blurted out, "How about the Drunken Queen Victoria?" in an unfunny and petty dig at my mother's . . . enthusiastic . . . drinking habits, to which she replied with a perfect, devastatingly polite dismissal: "Oh, but that doesn't make sense. Queen Victoria is on the Bombay Sapphire bottle, not Plymouth." She torched his ass.

Makes 1 drink

2 ounces **chilled soda water**

1½ ounces **Plymouth gin**

¾ ounce **fresh lemon juice**

½ ounce **Strega**

½ plus ⅛ ounce **Rothman & Winter Orchard Apricot brandy**

1 **egg white**

Suze, in a spray bottle, for finishing

Pour the soda into a chilled Collins or water glass. In a shaker, combine the remaining ingredients (except the Suze) and dry shake for 3 seconds. Add ice and shake again for 15 seconds. Strain into the prepared glass. Finish with a spray of Suze over the top.

Dry Prefecture

In 2013 I did a weeklong stint with Jim Meehan and Jeff Bell, another PDT bartender, at the Park Hyatt Tokyo's New York Bar—the bar made famous by *Lost in Translation*. We were tasked with creating a menu of Japan-themed drinks. I wanted to riff on the Dry County Cocktail at PDT, which is made with Tennessee whiskey, dry vermouth, and ginger liqueur. The drink is so named because its base spirit, whiskey, is produced in a "dry county" in Tennessee, where alcohol cannot be sold.

For my variation, I used Japanese whisky and changed the "county" to "prefecture," which is an administrative subunit of Japan somewhere between a county and a state. Witty, right? Shochu is a Japanese spirit made from such ingredients as sweet potato, sesame, and sugar, to name a few. Here I use barley shochu because its mellow graininess is a nice parallel to the whisky.

Makes 1 drink

2 ounces **barley shochu**

1 ounce **Japanese whisky, such as Suntory Hibiki**

½ ounce **Domaine de Canton**

Optional Garnish Candied ginger speared on a pick

In a mixing glass or shaking tin, combine the drink ingredients. Add ice and stir for 20 seconds. Strain into a chilled coupe. Garnish with a piece of candied ginger, if you like.

Supercharged Highball

In Japan you can buy Highballs in cans at every convenience store. Because of our liquor laws, this most likely will never be a thing in the United States. Fortunately for you, I exist and I created this recipe that will very closely approximate the experience of drinking a Highball from a can, where both the whiskey and the water are carbonated. And, because I'm a fancy boi, I start with sparkling mineral water instead of regular tap.

This drink will work with any type of carbonation equipment you have, as long as it has a bottle that holds at least a liter. If you need to scale the recipe to fit your equipment, just make sure you're keeping it at three parts water to one part whiskey. The drink will start to lose carbonation almost immediately, but it can be chilled and recarbonated indefinitely.

Makes about 4 drinks

7 ounces **Japanese whisky**

21 ounces **sparkling mineral water**

Garnishes Lemon wedges, grapefruit peels, or mint bouquet

Combine the whisky and sparkling water in a carbonation vessel and place it in the back of the refrigerator (where it's coldest) to chill for at least 2 hours.

Carbonate the drink according to the machine instructions. To serve, pour it into ice-filled water glasses. Garnish each glass with a lemon wedge, grapefruit peel, or mint leaf.

Kansai Kick

This drink came about relatively early in my bartending career at PDT. I initially wanted to use rye and dry vermouth in the recipe, but Jim Meehan, the bar's owner, suggested using Japanese whisky and Madeira as a way to incorporate fewer ingredients and add unexpected flavors, and it made my drink a million times better. Madeira comes from the Portuguese island of the same name and is made by heating wine and allowing it to age for ninety days. As a result of this process, the wine is essentially stable and will remain delicious and drinkable for a long time after the bottle is opened. Bual Madeira is a slightly sweeter style of Madeira. The rich, nutty flavors in this drink make it a perfect autumnal whiskey Daisy, though I drink it year-round.

Makes 1 drink

1½ ounces **Japanese whisky, such as Suntory Toki**

¾ ounce **fresh lime juice**

¾ ounce **Bual Madeira**

¾ ounce **Small Hand Foods orgeat**

In a shaker, combine the drink ingredients. Fill the shaker with ice and shake for 15 seconds. Strain into a chilled coupe.

Saffron Collins

Saffron is one of the fanciest food ingredients in the world. It must be painstakingly harvested by hand, by tweezing out the stigmas of a crocus blossom. But saffron is used in many foods: risotto, paella, and a number of amaros.* It's even been known to find its way into some gins.

For this drink you need just a few threads of saffron to impart its unique aroma of hay, honey, and, to some people, plastic. To make the drink truly fancy, use a high-end gin like Monkey 47 as your base, though another type of gin is acceptable, if you must.

But for the addition of saffron, this is a very classic Tom Collins recipe. For some mind-boggling reason, I think this drink tastes like Mountain Dew—if Mountain Dew cost $20 a can. It will make sense once you taste it.

Makes 1 drink

4 ounces / ½ cup **soda water**

1½ ounces **Saffron-Infused Gin** (recipe follows)

¾ ounce **fresh lemon juice**

¾ ounce **Simple Syrup** (page 68)

Garnish Lemon, Meyer lemon, or mandarin orange wheel

Pour 2 ounces of the soda water into an ice-filled Collins or water glass. In a shaking tin, combine the gin, lemon juice, and simple syrup. Dry shake for 5 seconds, then pour into the prepared glass. Top with the remaining 2 ounces soda water. Garnish with a citrus wheel.

SAFFRON-INFUSED GIN
Makes 6 ounces / ¾ cup

6 ounces / ¾ cup **gin, such as Monkey 47**

3 to 4 ½-inch-long **saffron threads**

In a medium container, combine the gin and saffron. Allow to infuse, covered, at room temperature overnight. Strain the gin through a gold coffee filter into a glass bottle, discarding the solids. Store in the bottle at room temperature indefinitely.

---

* There is an untrue myth (aren't they all untrue?) that the makers of Fernet-Branca buy 75% of the world's saffron supply, a fable debunked by Amy Stewart in *The Drunken Botanist*.

Sunrise Bloody Mary

One of my favorite places to seek inspiration is Sunrise Mart, a Japanese grocery store in New York City's East Village. After a recent visit, I left with the notion to make a Japanese Bloody Mary. If you visit a fancy cocktail bar in Japan and order a Bloody Mary, you'll simply get fresh tomato puréed with vodka. I wanted to re-create the airiness of the fresh tomato without having to go through the trouble of sourcing perfectly ripe and flavorful tomatoes, which is nearly impossible to do in New York City.

I added an egg yolk, whipping the drink in a blender to give the cocktail a rich, frothy texture. Japanese whisky is subbed for the traditional vodka, and soy sauce and *shichimi togarashi* give it heat and savory notes. (Shichimi togarashi is a blend of seven spices that typically includes sansho pepper, dried citrus peel, sesame seeds, poppy seeds, hemp seeds, ginger, garlic, shiso, and nori.) This is not quite the same as a true Japanese Bloody Mary, but it does replicate the texture of one.

Makes 2 drinks (because who wants to drink a Bloody Mary alone?)

16 ounces / 2 cups **tomato juice**

4 ounces / ½ cup **Japanese whisky**

½ ounce **high-quality soy sauce or usukuchi**

½ ounce **apple cider vinegar**

4 pinches **kosher salt**

4 pinches **shichimi togarashi**

10 turns of a **pepper mill**

1 **egg yolk**

1 cup **ice**

Optional Garnish Celery stalks

In a blender, combine the drink ingredients. Blend on high speed for 60 seconds, until smooth and frothy. Pour the drink into 2 old fashioned or water glasses. Garnish each drink with a celery stalk if that's your thing.

Sévérine

One of the joys of creating cocktails is that you can draw inspiration from so many places and things. Classic foods are a fallback source for me. Steak au poivre is one of the fanciest classic French dishes, made with Cognac and Cambodian Kampot black pepper. It's already got a spirit in there, so it follows logically to develop a recipe around it.

Another wonderful source of inspiration for cocktails is popular culture. One of the most famous fictional drinkers is James Bond. He is best known for drinking martinis, but there is also a classic martini variation named after Vesper, one of the original Bond Girls.

This drink draws upon both those sources.

Makes 1 drink

⅛ ounce **Suze**

6 **Kampot peppercorns** (see Note)

1½ ounces **vodka**

¾ ounce **Lillet blanc**

½ ounce **Cognac**

Garnish Lemon peel

In a mixing glass or shaking tin, combine the Suze and peppercorns. Muddle to crack open the peppercorns, then add the vodka, Lillet blanc, and Cognac. Add ice and stir for 15 seconds. Strain into a chilled coupe. Express a lemon peel over the surface of the drink, then discard the peel before serving.

NOTE Kampot peppercorns come from a specific region of Cambodia and have a more refined black pepper flavor than the standard; they are available online. This drink will work fine with the conventional stuff, however.

Coconut Old Fashioned

My favorite iteration of a fat wash-based cocktail is the Benton's Old Fashioned, which is made with bacon-infused bourbon and maple syrup. It's really hard to replicate the brilliance of that cocktail without being too much of a copycat, so I want to pay it proper homage by offering a more accessible (read: vegetarian) version. This recipe can serve as a template for any other fat washing you wish to do. This process can really smooth out some rough edges in a spirit—although the rum I like best for this drink, Mount Gay XO, doesn't really need any help in that regard. That's why I like it.

Makes 1 drink

2 ounces **Coconut Rum** (recipe follows)

¼ ounce **Demerara Syrup** (page 72)

4 dashes **Angostura bitters**

2 dashes **orange bitters**

Garnish Orange peel

In a mixing glass or shaking tin, combine the drink ingredients. Add ice and stir for 20 seconds. Strain into an ice-filled old fashioned glass. Garnish with an orange peel, expressed and then perched on the rim.

COCONUT RUM
Makes about 1½ cups

12 ounces / 1½ cups **aged rum** (I like Mount Gay XO)

1 ounce **virgin coconut oil**

In a medium airtight container, stir together the rum and coconut oil. Let the mixture sit, covered, at room temperature for at least 8 hours or overnight. Place the container in the freezer to chill for at least 2 hours; the fat should solidify into a cap on top of the rum. Skim off the layer of fat and strain the rum through a gold coffee filter into a glass bottle; discard the fat. Store in the bottle at room temperature for up to 2 months.

Baroque Daisy

This drink is just plain over the top—even for me. But also like me, it's worth the trouble.

The whiskey I recommend here, Stranahan's, is fantastic and not super cheap, but you should try to seek it out. It's made from malted barley, but it's aged in new oak, which is a hybrid of American and Scotch styles. Belle de Brillet is a fancy pear liqueur in a fancy pear-shaped bottle, and the Champagne syrup is a clever way to use any leftover—and perhaps flat—sparkling wine that might be taking up space in your fridge. What really makes this drink is the mist of Manzanilla sherry, which provides a complex, nutty prologue.

Makes 1 drink

1¼ ounces **Stranahan's Colorado Whiskey**

¾ ounce **Dead Champagne Syrup** (recipe follows)

½ ounce **Belle de Brillet**

¼ ounce **yuzu juice**

Garnish Manzanilla sherry, in a spray bottle

In a shaker, combine the drink ingredients. Add ice and shake for 15 seconds. Strain into a chilled coupe and garnish with a mist of sherry.

DEAD CHAMPAGNE SYRUP
Makes about 1½ cups

8 ounces / 1 cup **flat sparkling wine, preferably Champagne** (see Note)

1 cup **granulated sugar**

Combine the wine and sugar in a small bowl. Stir vigorously to combine. (You can use a blender if you want, but make sure the wine is really flat first, to avoid a Champagne supernova. Sorry.) Store in an airtight container in the refrigerator for up to 3 weeks or in the freezer for up to 6 months.

NOTE If your wine is not already flat, add a few spoonfuls of the sugar to the wine and stir. The wine will get super frothy and then die down. Add the remaining sugar.

Black Diamond

Despite the Japanese whisky here, the Black Diamond's inspiration actually comes from France—specifically, from the red wines of the Bordeaux region. I wanted to re-create their classic flavors—namely smoke, dark fruit, and a bit of spice. The result is an unexpected combination of whiskey, beer, and Bonal Quina, a French aromatized wine somewhat similar to vermouth. Don't think of this as a beer cocktail, though. The porter (you can use whatever's handy) will lose most of its fizz during the mixing and stirring.

Makes 1 drink

4 **fresh blackberries**

3 **black peppercorns**

1¾ ounces **Japanese whisky**

¾ ounce **Bonal Gentiane-Quina**

¾ ounce **porter beer**

¼ ounce **crème de cassis, such as Lejay**

In a mixing glass or straining tin, muddle 2 of the blackberries with the peppercorns until finely crushed. Add the remaining ingredients. Add ice and stir for 20 seconds. Fine-strain into a chilled coupe. Garnish with the remaining 2 blackberries speared on a pick.

FEELING FESTIVE

Whether it's a party of one or twenty, these drinks will help you go for it. They are here because they're either good for a party or they *are* the party. Like these drinks, the best parties have big, diverse—but harmonious—guest lists, are intellectually engaging, and crackle with vibrant, joyful energy.

Aggressively Simple Vodka Punch

Punches are a type of batched cocktail that takes a lot of pressure off the person making them. You basically throw all the ingredients into a bowl and walk away. This method is great at a party because you can have a good time (or find something else to worry about) while your guests serve themselves. And since you've dropped a few large blocks of ice in the bowl along with everything else, the drink stays cool and actually gets weaker as time goes on, which is a nice way to prevent your friends (or yourself) from getting too hammered on a Sunday afternoon and blacking out before *Westworld.**

I call this drink the Aggressively Simple Vodka Punch because it's so simple and easy, both to make and to drink. Consider it your training-wheels punch if you're a first-timer. You'll need a large container to mix it in and a large bowl to serve it in. A plain kitchen mixing bowl works well, but if you want to make a commitment, it's not hard to find a cute punch bowl. Although, depending on the size of your bowl, you may need to keep any excess punch in the fridge and replenish as people drink.

NOTE Use sparkling water in place of the sparkling wine if you want to keep your punch low-ABV. And if you want to get fancy, use an infused syrup like mint or basil instead of the plain simple syrup.

---

* Just me? Okay.

Serves about 12

12 ounces / 1½ cups **vodka**

12 ounces / 1½ cups **St-Germain**

8 ounces / 1 cup **fresh lemon juice**

4 ounces / ½ cup **fresh lime juice**

8 ounces / 1 cup **grapefruit juice**

8 ounces / 1 cup **Simple Syrup** (page 68)

12 ounces / 1½ cups **sparkling wine, such as Cava or Prosecco**

1 **English cucumber,** peeled and thinly sliced

4 **ice blocks** (recipe follows)

Combine the vodka, St-Germain, citrus juices, and simple syrup in a large bowl or a 4-quart Cambro, and stir to combine. If you have time, let the mixture chill in the refrigerator for an hour or two.

Transfer the mixture to a punch bowl and add the sparkling wine, cucumber slices, and ice blocks. Perch a ladle on the side of the bowl and walk away from the punch or the whole party— up to you.

ICE BLOCKS

Makes 4 blocks

Fill four 1-pint containers three-quarters full with filtered water. Place the containers, uncovered, in the freezer and leave until the blocks are frozen, about 10 hours.

To use, remove the containers from the freezer, let them thaw for 2 to 3 minutes, and then pop the blocks out of the containers and into the punch bowl. *Hot tip: Use Bundt cake molds as your container.*

The Shark

The Shark might be the most notorious cocktail I've ever created. I initially wanted to make a tiki drink that was suitable for the winter—something with rich flavors but not explicitly fruity in the way many tiki drinks are.

I was working on it with Jim Meehan at PDT, tweaking levels of various sweeteners and fruit juices to get the balance right. When I told Jim I was playing around with apricot liqueur, he scrunched up his face in his classic fashion and said, "No." He told me that apricot isn't tiki, and advised me to instead use orange curaçao. To which I replied—fully joking—"How about *blue* curaçao?" Well, he called my bluff. After that, another colleague took one sip and said, "This needs a quarter ounce of cream." It turns out that was the keystone ingredient that tied everything together: the cream moderated the drink's blue hue, added a bit of fluffy texture, and softened the acidity from the pineapple, lemon juice, and curaçao.

Makes 4 drinks

6 ounces / ¾ cup **Butter-Infused Rum** (recipe on page 156)

3 ounces **overproof Jamaican rum, such as Wray & Nephew**

2 ounces **blue curaçao**

2 ounces **Frangelico hazelnut liqueur**

1½ ounces **cane syrup**

3 ounces **fresh lemon juice**

1½ ounces **pineapple juice**

1 ounce **heavy cream**

⅛ ounce **Bittermen's 'Elemakule Tiki Bitters**

2 cups **ice cubes**

Garnishes Lemon wheels and cocktail umbrellas

In a blender, combine the drink ingredients. Blend on medium speed until smooth, about 30 seconds. Pour into chilled old fashioned glasses and garnish each one with a lemon wheel. Add a cocktail umbrella and serve with a straw.

155 ➡

BUTTER-INFUSED RUM
Makes about 12 ounces / 1½ cups

12 ounces / 1½ cups **white rum, such as Banks 5 Island or Flor de Caña 4-year**

4 tablespoons (½ stick) **unsalted butter, melted**

In a medium airtight container, combine the rum and butter. Let the mixture sit at room temperature, covered, for at least 8 hours, or overnight. Transfer it to the freezer to chill for at least 1 hour, until the butter has solidified.

Pour the infused rum through a gold coffee filter into an airtight container, discarding the solids. Store in the refrigerator for up to 1 month or in the freezer for up to 6 months.

NOTE At PDT, this drink is served over pebble ice. Most people do not have access to this kind of ice at home, so I've adapted the recipe for use in a blender and scaled it up so that it serves four people. Drinks made in a blender tend to be more diluted and much colder than shaken and stirred drinks, so they're balanced slightly differently. They need to be sweeter—otherwise they taste thin.

Pineapple Scotch Punch

This punch is intermediate level in terms of both preparation and palate. On paper, you might not think these ingredients go together, but they do. I've found the combination of Scotch and pineapple to be very compelling, with a degree of aromatic overlap that allows the rounder, honey-inflected flavors in the pineapple to draw out certain similar fruity flavors in the Scotch. The inclusion of Drambuie—a Scotch, honey, and clove liqueur—is a callback to the classic cocktail the Rusty Nail. The dry vermouth works to brighten and provide additional complexity. Topping off the drink with apricot-flavored seltzer supports the Scotch/pineapple combination, due to its round fruitiness. You can use regular sparkling water if that's your preference.

Serves about 12

12 ounces / 1½ cups **blended Scotch whisky**

5 ounces **French dry vermouth**

8 ounces / 1 cup **Drambuie**

10 ounces / 1¼ cups **pineapple juice**

4 ounces / ½ cup **fresh lemon juice**

6 to 8 **lemon wheels**

30 **whole cloves**

2 (12-ounce) cans **chilled apricot seltzer, such as La Croix**

2 **ice blocks** (page 153)

In a large bowl or a 4-quart Cambro, combine the Scotch, vermouth, Drambuie, pineapple juice, and lemon juice and stir to combine. If you have time, let the mixture chill in the refrigerator for an hour or two.

For each lemon wheel, press the pointy end of 4 or 5 cloves into the fruit in a circular pattern. Transfer the lemon wheels to the punch bowl and add the Scotch mixture, seltzer, and ice blocks. Perch a ladle on the side of the bowl and walk away from your entire life.

Singapore Sling

In the canon of reasonably well-known classic cocktails, the Singapore Sling gets the least amount of play. It's never been the subject of a breathless trend piece, and that's a damn shame. This drink is awesome. It's got something for everyone—it's fruity, intriguing and slightly bitter, and surprisingly strong.* Allegedly the drink was created in Singapore at the Raffles Hotel's Long Bar, and it would be appropriate for such a refreshing drink to originate in a place that clocks in at 90°F with 65% humidity, 365 days per year. But if you actually look into the history, the story starts to fall apart. Honestly, who cares.

There seems to be no standard recipe for the drink. Case in point: I went to Raffles Hotel in 2013 and was served, in immediate succession, the best and then the worst Singapore Slings I've had in my life. This is the recipe that I find to be the most delicious. It's strong, complex, and extremely refreshing—perfect on a hot and steamy summer evening.

Makes 1 drink

1½ ounces **navy-strength gin, such as Plymouth**

1½ ounces **pineapple juice**

½ ounce **Cherry Heering**

½ ounce **Grenadine** (page 129)

¼ ounce **Cointreau**

¼ ounce **Bénédictine**

¼ ounce **fresh lime juice**

2 dashes **Angostura bitters**

Garnishes Pineapple wedge and Luxardo cherry

In a shaker, combine the drink ingredients. Add ice and shake for 15 seconds. Strain into an ice-filled Collins or water glass. Garnish with the pineapple wedge and a cherry speared on a pick. Serve with a straw.

NOTE I find that using a high-proof, or navy-strength, gin makes the juniper notes pop, giving the drink the best aromatic balance, but you can use regular gin if you prefer.

---

* Like me.

Weed Punch*

My husband and I throw a party every year that is kind of a mash-up of Halloween and Christmas, in both timing and theme. I ~~prance~~ wobble around, incapacitatingly high on MDMA, in a Santa Claus cloak while wearing a jock strap, red fishnet stockings, and six-inch heels. Needless to say, this party is debauched. (You literally can't spell "debauchery" without "deBary," by the way.) But why stop there? I thought it a wise idea to make a punch with weed-infused absinthe. If that does not scream "party," I don't know what does.

The only problem, I find, with edible weed is that it generally is not appetizing. It kinda tastes like burnt skunky grass, which, well, it is. I use weed-compatible flavors—green and vegetal—to mask the skunk by bundling it up with similar but tastier things. Think of it as hiding a wilted flower amongst a bouquet of fresh ones. You can apply this strategy anywhere you're dealing with a challenging flavor that you're looking to integrate into something more accessible.

NOTE The thing about weed infusions is that you can't just toss the dry weed into something and call it a day. Well, you can, but the psychoactive molecule won't be active and you'll just have weed-flavored spirits. You need to heat it to about 220°F in order for it to have the desired effect.

---

* I am of the belief that weed should be legal everywhere. In certain places in the United States it is, and this recipe is only for people who are in those states.

Serves about 12

6 ounces / ¾ cup **Weed-Infused Absinthe** (recipe follows)

6 ounces / ¾ cup **gin**

4 ounces / ½ cup **fresh lime juice**

4 ounces / ½ cup **Mint Simple Syrup** (page 125)

16 ounces / 2 cups **sparkling water**

1 (750mL) bottle **sparkling wine**

2 large **ice blocks** (page 153)

1 **English cucumber,** peeled and thinly sliced

In a large bowl or a 4-quart Cambro, combine the weed absinthe, gin, lime juice, and mint simple syrup and stir together. If you have time, let the mixture chill in the refrigerator for an hour or two.

Transfer the mixture to a punch bowl and pour in the sparkling water and sparkling wine. Add the ice blocks and cucumber slices. Perch a ladle on the side of the bowl and don't walk away. You need to keep an eye on your friends for this one.

WEED-INFUSED ABSINTHE
Makes 6 to 7 ounces

600mg **marijuana,** crumbled

8 ounces / 1 cup **absinthe, such as St. George**

Preheat the oven to 220°F.

Place the marijuana in a small oven-safe saucepan, cover it, and heat in the oven for 1 hour. The weed might look slightly brown but shouldn't look burnt.

In a double boiler, or in a large metal bowl set over a medium-size pot of simmering water, combine the toasted marijuana and the absinthe. Cover the bowl loosely with aluminum foil and cook for 15 minutes. Remove the bowl from the heat and let it sit at room temperature for 1 hour.

Strain the infused absinthe through a gold coffee filter into a glass container, discarding the solids. Use immediately or store the container at room temperature for up to 1 year.

Legit Eggnog

I serve this eggnog to my family every year at Christmas Eve dinner. It's perfect with the *bûche de Noël* I make, which is a tradition I inherited from my mother. I tend to make the eggnog pretty strong, and since I will have been cooking for the past three days straight, I have a glass or two and promptly pass out. (Passing out at your own dinner party is the level of Waspy dominance that I'm proud to have achieved more than a few times.)

This recipe is very forgiving. Feel free to tweak the spirits based on your preferences and on what you have lying around. You can essentially free-pour this drink in a hurry, tasting as you go—the balance does not hang on a razor's edge. The fat content from the cream and eggs smooths over any roughness.

Serves about 10

12 **jumbo eggs,** separated

8 ounces / 1 cup **navy-strength rum, such as Smith & Cross**

8 ounces / 1 cup **bourbon**

8 ounces / 1 cup **Cognac**

8 ounces / 1 cup **heavy cream**

6 ounces / ¾ cup **grade B maple syrup**

3 **whole nutmeg seeds**

In a medium bowl, beat the egg whites until stiff peaks form.

In a large bowl, beat the yolks with the rum, bourbon, Cognac, cream, and maple syrup until everything is incorporated. Using a Microplane, grate the whole nuts of meg into the yolk mixture. Gently fold the whites into the mixture. Pour the eggnog into an airtight container and chill it in the refrigerator for at least 3 hours.

I like to serve this in little teacups.

NOTE You can make this eggnog up to 1 week in advance. The more time the eggnog has to chill, the more the flavors integrate.

FEELING SOBER

Making drinks without alcohol is challenging. In a way, using spirits and other alcohol-containing things is cheating since they contain such an abundance of deliciousness and are easily mixed. When excluding alcohol, you have to come up with clever tricks to incorporate the flavors you want and find ingredients you can rely on to make the drink feel sophisticated.

More often than not, alcohol-free cocktails are sadly overlooked, both by bars and restaurants and by patrons who might turn up their noses at something that won't give them a buzz for their buck. Although, as more and more people are drinking less, that's changing.

These recipes are about giving you options. Maybe you don't drink at all, maybe you don't feel like it at the moment—whatever. Not drinking doesn't always have to be a *thing*. Live your life; drink what you want.

Morning Mai Tai

I'll never forget the time I visited Japan with my family when I was thirteen years old and saw two elegantly dressed Japanese women pounding beers with their breakfast in our hotel lobby. Since we all can't go through life like those icons, it's good to have a few alcohol-free beverages to awaken our senses in the morning.

A classic mai tai is a mix of rum with orgeat, a Middle Eastern almond syrup, and other flavors. To re-create it as a safe-for-the-morning cocktail, I've used apple cider paired with ginger to echo the rich and spicy notes from the rum. Apple cider vinegar, if used judiciously, provides an eye-opening dose of acidity, along with additional apple notes.

Makes 1 drink

1½ ounces **chilled apple cider**

½ ounce **apple cider vinegar**

½ ounce **Ginger Syrup** (page 106)

½ ounce **orgeat**

Garnishes Apple slices and fresh mint leaves

In a shaking tin, combine the drink ingredients. Add ice and shake for 15 seconds. Strain into an ice-filled old fashioned glass. Garnish with a few slices of apple and a couple of mint leaves.

Raspberry-Jalapeño Fizz

This drink is all about the interplay of jalapeño, banana, and raspberry, which is an unexpected but excellent combination. The lime juice balances out the sweetness in the raspberry preserves and banana, jalapeño offers a replacement for alcoholic heat, and verjus—the acidic juice of unripe wine grapes—is the base that we're building all these flavors onto. I love verjus because it has a depth and complexity that regular grape juice can't even begin to approach.

Makes 1 drink

Lime wedge

Kosher salt

1 thin, seeded slice of **jalapeño**

1 (1-inch-thick) slice of **ripe banana**

1½ ounces **chilled verjus, such as Wölffer Estate**

½ ounce **raspberry preserves**

¾ ounce **fresh lime juice**

1½ ounces **sparkling water**

Use the lime wedge to moisten the rim of a chilled coupe, and then dip one side of the rim into salt to coat it. Place the glass in the freezer to chill for 10 minutes.

Combine the jalapeño and banana in a shaking tin and muddle together until the jalapeño is crushed. Add the verjus, raspberry preserves, and lime juice. Add ice and shake for 15 seconds. Fine-strain into the prepared glass and top with the sparkling water.

Lapsang Old Fashioned

Lapsang Souchong tea leaves are made by drying *Camellia sinensis* leaves over a wood fire. In addition to being an objectively delicious stand-alone beverage, the tea is also great when mixed into cocktails. Its smokiness imparts a sophisticated whiskey-like character. Here it's cold brewed, a technique I use because it results in a rounder, fuller flavor and because the tea stays stable for quite a while, as opposed to hot brewed tea, which is good for only a few hours.

This drink loosely resembles an Old Fashioned, with the tea acting as the spirit base while the black pepper syrup and maple syrup act as the sweeteners. The black pepper syrup also re-creates the heat that people associate with spirits.

Makes 1 drink

6 ounces / ¾ cup **Cold Brew Lapsang Souchong Tea** (recipe follows)

½ ounce **Black Pepper Syrup** (page 173)

¼ ounce **grade B maple syrup**

Garnish Lemon peel

Combine the drink ingredients in an ice-filled old fashioned glass and stir briefly. Garnish with a lemon peel.

COLD BREW LAPSANG SOUCHONG TEA
Makes about 4 cups

20g / about ½ cup **loose Lapsang Souchong tea leaves**

4 cups **filtered water**

In a medium airtight container or a 4-quart Cambro, stir the tea leaves into the water. Cover and place the container in the refrigerator to infuse for 8 hours or overnight.

Strain the tea through a gold coffee filter into an airtight container, discarding the solids. Store, covered, in the refrigerator for up to 2 weeks.

Licorice Hot Toddy

Licorice tea has an extra-special, hard-to-describe chewy/sweet texture—and not as much of an anise/fennel note as you might expect. Brew a mug of it straight and you'd swear there was sugar in it. I rely on licorice tea a lot in alcohol-free cocktails. Its complex character makes the drink feel more adult and sophisticated.

The combination of ginger and black pepper syrups here replicates some of the heat and edge that's lost by omitting alcohol and balances the soft, sweet notes from the licorice. Don't neglect the lemon wedge—the slight hit of acidity brightens the drink and balances some of the sweetness.

Makes 1 drink

2 **licorice tea bags**

¼ ounce **Ginger Syrup** (page 106)

¼ ounce **Black Pepper Syrup** (recipe follows)

8 ounces / 1 cup **boiling filtered water**

Garnish Lemon wedge

Combine the tea bags, ginger syrup, and black pepper syrup in a mug, and pour in the boiling water. Let steep for 4 to 5 minutes, then discard the tea bags. Garnish with the lemon wedge.

BLACK PEPPER SYRUP
Makes about 6 ounces / ¾ cup

¼ cup **freshly ground black pepper**

8 ounces / 1 cup **filtered water**

1 cup **granulated sugar**

In a blender, combine all the ingredients and blend on high speed for 2 minutes, until the sugar has dissolved completely. Strain through a gold coffee filter into an airtight container, discarding the solids. Store in the refrigerator for up to 2 weeks or in the freezer for up to 6 months.

Sunday Morning Royale

I admittedly had a pretty posh upbringing, part of which included a formal Sunday Morning Breakfast™ every week. It would start with fresh grapefruit, continue with eggs and bacon, and finish with coffee cake or muffins. I thought this was normal for a lot longer than I should have.* As a result, I have a fondness for grapefruit and grapefruit juice—I made fresh grapefruit juice for the family every Christmas morning until my mother died and my dad sold the house.

This drink is in honor of my mother, and in honor of our breakfast tradition. It's based around the acidity and slight bitterness of red grapefruit paired with the white pepper fennel syrup. Fennel and grapefruit isn't the most common matchup, but the duo provides a complex, adult sensibility. White pepper supplies a gentler heat than black pepper, and the raspberry preserves gives a pop of sweetness and a lush texture.

---

* It's not not normal, but it's also not normal.

Makes 1 drink

1½ ounces **fresh red grapefruit juice**

½ ounce **White Pepper Fennel Syrup** (recipe follows)

1 tablespoon **raspberry preserves**

3 ounces **chilled Italian grapefruit soda, such as S.Pellegrino**

2 ounces **chilled grapefruit-flavored or plain sparkling water**

In a shaker, combine the grapefruit juice, white pepper fennel syrup, and raspberry preserves. Dry shake for 3 seconds. Pour the Italian grapefruit soda into an ice-filled Collins or water glass. Add the contents of the shaker, and top with the sparkling water. Serve with a straw.

WHITE PEPPER FENNEL SYRUP

Makes about 2 cups

1 cup **sugar**

8 ounces / 1 cup **filtered water**

2 cups chopped **fresh fennel bulb**

2 tablespoons **whole white peppercorns**

2 tablespoons **fennel seeds**

In a blender, combine all the ingredients and blend on high speed for 2 minutes, until the sugar has dissolved. Strain through a gold coffee filter into an airtight container, discarding the solids. Store in the refrigerator for up to 2 weeks or in the freezer for up to 6 months.

Black Pineapple Elixir

Consider this drink something of an alcohol-free gin and tonic substitute—a fairly simple cocktail that offers a great deal of complexity. The bitter tonic and sweet, fruity pineapple balance each other out, while the black pepper syrup supplies that spicy kick that's too often missing from alcohol-free cocktails.

Makes 1 drink

2 ounces **pineapple juice**

½ ounce **Black Pepper Syrup** (page 173)

4 ounces / ½ cup **tonic water, such as Fever-Tree or Whole Foods 365 brand**

Optional Garnish Wedge of pineapple

Pour the pineapple juice, black pepper syrup, and 2 ounces of the tonic water into an ice-filled Collins or water glass, and stir to combine. Top up with the remaining 2 ounces tonic water, and garnish with a pineapple wedge if you like.

Watermelon Fennel Collins

A more perfect drink does not exist for a sultry, sweaty late afternoon in summer. White pepper is an excellent way to re-create the heat and spice that spirits provide, while the fresh fennel and fennel seed in the syrup allude to spirits like gin and absinthe. Pairing these flavors with watermelon is unexpected, but it's surprisingly tasty and sophisticated.

This drink can be easily spiked with vodka, gin, or blanco tequila, and it works well scaled up as a pitcher drink (with or without spirits). Bring a couple of bottles to your next barbecue and everyone will love you.

Makes 1 drink

4 ounces / ½ cup **sparkling water**

3 ounces fresh **watermelon juice**

1 ounce **White Pepper Fennel Syrup** (page 175)

Garnish Lime wedge

Fill a water glass with ice and pour in 2 ounces of the sparkling water. Add the watermelon juice and white pepper fennel syrup, then add the remaining 2 ounces sparkling water. Give a stir to combine. Garnish with a lime wedge, and serve with a straw.

Botanical Cold Brew

I love making cold brew coffee because I am a lazy piece of shit in the morning and the last thing I want to do is wrestle with some janky coffeemaker contraption and have to wait for the coffee to drip down.* With cold brew, you just microwave a half-full mug of water with a few ounces of the coffee concentrate for ninety seconds. It's so easy and fast, and the concentrate keeps in the fridge for weeks. And you can even freeze it into ice cubes for the best iced coffee ever.

Even though you can buy concentrate premade, I consider it wasteful, so I make my own. One day I got bored with plain coffee and started playing around with the excessive number of herbs and spices in my pantry. I started with Ceylon cinnamon and nutmeg to add depth, and added the cloves to complement the coffee's aromatics and provide some tones to balance what's deep and dark. The chili powder was kind of a "fuck it, let's see what happens" move. It was an attempt to hark back to ancient Aztec traditions of spicy, savory hot chocolate. It worked. It makes the coffee pop without making it spicy.

NOTE You'll need special equipment to make cold brew easily. You can buy something called the Toddy Cold Brew System, which is relatively inexpensive and has everything you need to get your cold brew situation up and running. If you're not sure you want to commit just yet, follow the instructions here, using a large container like a 4-quart Cambro or even a large mixing bowl. The challenge will be straining the coffee after the brew is over. I would recommend first straining it through a large metal strainer to get the large grounds separated out, and then straining it again through a gold coffee filter to capture the fine particles. You can store the concentrate in the refrigerator for up to 1 month—or freeze it into ice cubes, for up to 6 months—to enjoy the best iced coffee of your life.

---

* Yeah, yeah, I know about pour-over, but even that's too much work for me—you have to boil water!

Makes about 7 cups

9 cups **filtered water**

1 pound **coarsely ground medium-roast coffee**

¼ cup **whole cloves**

¼ teaspoon **chili powder**

2 **whole nutmeg seeds, ground**

2 (2-inch) sticks **Ceylon cinnamon, crumbled**

Pour 2 cups of the water into the coffee Toddy, a large mixing bowl, or a 4-quart Cambro. Cover the water with ½ pound of the ground coffee. Add the cloves, chili powder, nutmeg, and cinnamon, and then top with an additional 5 cups of the water. Add the remaining ½ pound coffee, then the remaining 2 cups water. Let sit at room temperature for at least 12 hours.

Strain the cold brew into a large jar or other container (see Note).

To serve, combine ¼ cup of the cold brew with 1 cup of filtered water in a mug. Heat in the microwave for 90 seconds.

FEELING DESPERATE

We've all been there. Desperation is about making compromises in order to make the best of a sub-optimal situation. The drinks in this chapter are examples of how to compromise intelligently, using what you have on hand to make drinks that are still great. The fun thing about desperation is that it forces us to be creative, to find solutions where we might not have thought to look. What's important here is that we never lose sight of what makes an objectively delicious cocktail: all of these recipes abide by the same tenets of balance as the rest of the recipes in this book. The fun part here is that, since you're in dire straits, the surprise that you can throw together a legit cocktail is a big part of your subjective enjoyment.

Melted Firecracker Margarita

Imagine you're picnicking at the beach or in a park, the ice cream truck rolls up, and you're feeling frisky. Most treats are ice-cream-based and it's hard to make a tasty cocktail out of them. But the Firecracker Popsicle is icy. It's a classic—and a sure thing on that truck. Its icy-sour-sweet combination of flavors plays well with some tequila on a hot summer day.

This recipe is an example of using already-balanced off-the-shelf ingredients when you either don't want to, or can't, make everything from scratch. Since someone already did the work of concocting the Firecracker with the right balance of sugar and acidity, you won't have to tinker with any of that. I'm assuming you didn't bring a shaker to this picnic, so get creative—use two empty deli containers or plastic cups, and save the wooden ice pop sticks to be your stirrers.

Makes 1 drink

2 **Firecracker Popsicles**

1 ounce **blanco tequila** (but let's assume you're free-pouring)

Let the pops thaw enough so that you can pull the sticks out, using the wrapper as a sheath. Transfer the pops to a shaking vessel. Add the tequila and shake until the mixture is consistently slushy and intensely purple. Serve with a straw.

Alternatively, you can pour some tequila into a Solo cup and let the pops melt into it, if you're looking to truly do the least amount of work.

Honeysuckle

This drink is one of gentle desperation. You'll need access to honey and fresh citrus, but you can throw in literally any base spirit you have lying around. Sometimes the right spirit is the one you happen to have with you. The drink works because the base ingredients, lime and honey, are malleable enough to adapt to the spirit. That said, my favorites for this drink are rum, gin, and tequila.

Makes 1 drink

2 ounces **base spirit**

¾ ounce **fresh lime juice**

¾ ounce **Honey Syrup** (recipe follows)

In a shaker, combine the drink ingredients. Add ice and shake for 15 seconds. Strain into a chilled coupe.

HONEY SYRUP
Makes about 1 cup

¾ cup **honey**

6 ounces / ¾ cup **warm filtered water**

In a medium bowl, whisk together the honey and warm water. Let the mixture cool completely before using. Store in an airtight container in the refrigerator for up to 2 weeks or in the freezer for up to 6 months.

Desperation Flip

There comes a point in every person's life when they know enough to think they can do anything but they don't know enough to know what their limitations are, and they get cocky. Maybe they take up a new hobby or advance up the ladder at work. For me it was at a friend's party. I wanted to show off my prowess and make the group some cocktails. I had been bartending for a few months and knew enough about the mechanics of cocktails but had not yet come to fully understand just how much preparation and forethought goes into them.

I managed to pull off this very decent cocktail using what my friend had lying around, including holding a mug and a pint glass together as a shaker, even though it might have been a bit messy. And as it turns out, a flip is one of the most primordial cocktails there is, drunk centuries ago as a breakfast pick-me-up.

Makes 1 drink

2 (ish) ounces **dark rum**
¾ (ish) ounce **maple syrup**
1 **large egg**

In a shaker (or whatever you're using to shake), combine the drink ingredients. Dry shake for 5 seconds. Add ice and shake for 15 seconds. Strain into a chilled glass.

NOTE Full disclosure: I free-pour this cocktail. Like eggnog, it's pretty forgiving, so it will still work if you use approximate measures in your desperation.

Room-Temperature Flask Cocktail

Most cocktails rely on the fact that cold temperatures diminish the sensation of alcohol, reduce aromatics, and downplay sweetness. But what to do if you don't have a way to keep things cool and you want to drink on the go? An insulated water bottle won't always provide adequate discretion, so sometimes it's best to rely on the trusty flask. Of course, you can always fill a flask with whiskey, vodka, or gin (or Kahlúa—I don't judge), but drinking warm spirits this way is not always everyone's first choice. So what can you do to make a stiff warm drink a bit more palatable?

For ambient-temperature cocktails, you want to avoid citrus, as the temperature makes the acidity overpowering—and here it brings out the herbal complexities in the Campari and vermouth. You'll also want to lower the proof a bit since the presence of alcohol is much more apparent at warmer temperatures. This recipe assumes a flask capacity of 8 ounces (1 cup), so check and scale accordingly.

Makes enough to fill 1 (8-ounce) flask

1½ ounces **bourbon**
1½ ounces **sweet vermouth**
1½ ounces **Campari**
¾ ounce **crème de cacao**
1½ ounces **filtered water**

Pour all the ingredients into your flask and give it a little shake to combine.

NOTE You can also make these drinks non-flasky and serve them in wine glasses as a nightcap.

At Your In-Laws' Cocktail Flowchart

Here is what I hope is a useful tool for the next time you come across a musty and neglected liquor cabinet, whether you're actually at your in-laws' or not. It assumes that there aren't any perishable alcohol-containing liquids such as wine, vermouth, or sherry, but that you do have access to kitchen basics. This might be a time where you use something else besides a shaker to shake: a mason jar, a quart container, a mug and a glass held together—feel free to get creative and don't be afraid to make a mess. And it should go without saying that you can always pour something out neat, on the rocks, or even as a Highball if you have access to bubbles. You're not going to win an award for any drink you make using this guide, but it should enable you to do a little more than you thought you could, which is all that matters.

LIQUEUR SOUR

2 oz **liqueur**
1 oz **fresh lemon juice**
1 **egg white,** if you have it

Combine ingredients in a shaker, shake without ice for 5 seconds, add ice, and shake again for 15 seconds. Strain.

LIQUEUR SHRUB

1.5 oz **fruit liqueur**
0.5 oz **apple cider vinegar**
4-5 oz **sparkling water**

Combine ingredients in an ice-filled water glass.

SIMPLER MODIFIED SOUR

1.5 oz **base spirit**
1 oz **liqueur**
0.75 oz **fresh lemon or lime juice**

Combine ingredients in a shaker, add ice, and shake for 15 seconds. Strain into a glass.

DESPERATION STIRRED DRINK

2 oz **bourbon**
0.75 oz **crème de pêche**
0.5 oz **Bénédictine**

Combine ingredients in an ice-filled old fashioned glass. Stir for 10 seconds.

Deep breaths. Open liquor cabinet and take stock.

Are there any base spirits: gin, rum, brandy, whiskey, etc.? What about liqueurs?

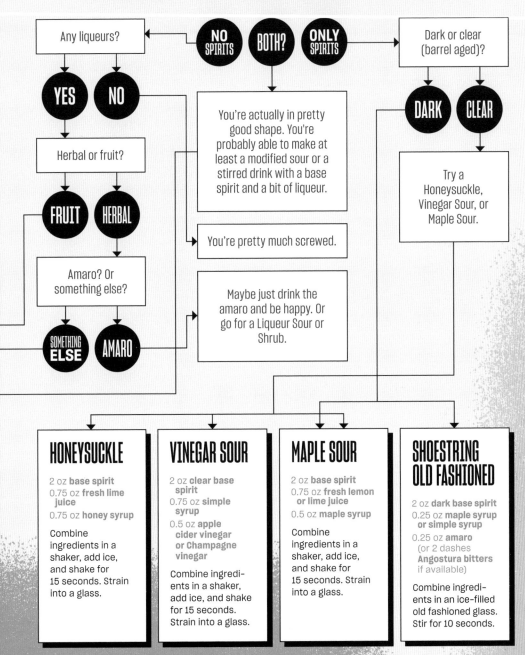

Any liqueurs?

NO SPIRITS · **BOTH?** · **ONLY SPIRITS**

Dark or clear (barrel aged)?

YES · **NO**

You're actually in pretty good shape. You're probably able to make at least a modified sour or a stirred drink with a base spirit and a bit of liqueur.

DARK · **CLEAR**

Herbal or fruit?

Try a Honeysuckle, Vinegar Sour, or Maple Sour.

FRUIT · **HERBAL**

You're pretty much screwed.

Amaro? Or something else?

Maybe just drink the amaro and be happy. Or go for a Liqueur Sour or Shrub.

SOMETHING ELSE · **AMARO**

HONEYSUCKLE

2 oz **base spirit**
0.75 oz **fresh lime juice**
0.75 oz **honey syrup**

Combine ingredients in a shaker, add ice, and shake for 15 seconds. Strain into a glass.

VINEGAR SOUR

2 oz **clear base spirit**
0.75 oz **simple syrup**
0.5 oz **apple cider vinegar or Champagne vinegar**

Combine ingredients in a shaker, add ice, and shake for 15 seconds. Strain into a glass.

MAPLE SOUR

2 oz **base spirit**
0.75 oz **fresh lemon or lime juice**
0.5 oz **maple syrup**

Combine ingredients in a shaker, add ice, and shake for 15 seconds. Strain into a glass.

SHOESTRING OLD FASHIONED

2 oz **dark base spirit**
0.25 oz **maple syrup or simple syrup**
0.25 oz **amaro** (or 2 dashes **Angostura bitters** if available)

Combine ingredients in an ice-filled old fashioned glass. Stir for 10 seconds.

191

Wine Sours

Wine offers a surprising amount of mileage as a beverage. Of course, you can drink and cook with wine, but you might not know that it's also a great source of acidity and flavor in cocktails. I can imagine plenty of situations where you'd want to use wine in a cocktail: you have a box of bleh wine that you want to use up; you can't or don't want to juice citrus; or you want to impress someone by showing them how resourceful you are—it's a neat trick.

Structurally, wine-based cocktails look very different from your classic sours or Manhattans. With these examples, notice the pattern of using 1 to 2 (or 3) ounces of wine, plus an ounce of base spirit, and occasionally a sweetener. This pattern is super riffable, so you'll be all set the next time you need to whip up a fancy cocktail out of thin air.

Each recipe makes 1 drink

1½ ounces **red wine**	1½ ounces **white wine**	3 ounces **white wine**	2 ounces **red wine**	3 ounces **white wine**
1 ounce **white rum**	1 ounce **bourbon**	½ ounce **St-Germain**	1 ounce **Frangelico hazelnut liqueur**	1 ounce **Amaretto liqueur**
½ ounce **Simple Syrup** (page 68)	½ ounce **orange curaçao**	½ ounce **Honey Syrup** (page 186)		

Choose a sour and combine all the ingredients in a shaker. Add ice and shake vigorously for 15 seconds. Strain into a chilled coupe.

NOTE I use very middle-of-the road French table wines for these, but they should work with most still wines. I would stay away from very sweet Rieslings or funky natural wines.

Vinegar Sours

It's fairly ubiquitous, keeps virtually forever, and offers a distinct flavor: vinegar is an excellent pantry item to have on hand for whenever the mood for a zingy non-citrus cocktail strikes you. Do the work to seek out and determine your favorite vinegars; stock two or three that you like, and you'll be set for a while. Apple cider vinegar is an excellent standby that's fairly easy to find—I like Bragg. Fruit vinegars, made by macerating fruit and sugar into vinegar, come in a variety of flavors. Dry vinegars do not have any added sugar but may be flavored with ingredients like lemon, honey, or fig. I've been using the O brand vinegars for years in a number of successful cocktails. Just one thing: please do not use distilled white vinegar—it's disgusting in cocktails.

Enjoy these three recipes as they are, but also consider them as frameworks for your own creativity.

Each recipe makes 1 drink

Fruit Vinegar Sour

1½ ounces **bourbon**

½ ounce **raspberry vinegar (I like Huilerie Beaujolaise)**

½ ounce **grade B maple syrup**

In a shaker, combine the drink ingredients. Add ice and shake for 15 seconds. Strain into a chilled coupe.

Dry Vinegar Sour

2 ounces **gin**

¾ ounce **Simple Syrup** (page 68)

½ ounce **citrus Champagne vinegar, such as O brand**

In a shaker, combine the drink ingredients. Add ice and shake for 15 seconds. Strain into a chilled coupe.

Liqueur Shrub

4 ounces / ½ cup **sparkling water**

1½ ounces **fruit liqueur, such as Cointreau or crème de pêche**

½ ounce **apple cider vinegar**

Pour 1 ounce of the sparkling water into an ice-filled water or Collins glass. Add the liqueur and vinegar. Top with the remaining 3 ounces sparkling water.

Ketchup Michelada

By definition, a michelada is a cocktail of hot sauce, beer, and lime; it is delightful when made with the proper care and preparation. This is not that michelada. We're using ketchup here because it is a ubiquitous, beloved condiment. It's sweet, but with enough acidity to balance out that sweetness, plus a fair helping of salt. This recipe also calls for hot sauce, since hot sauce improves pretty much everything; but if you don't have it around or don't want to use it, that's fine.

I don't expect anyone to make this drink on purpose. That means that I hope no one sets out to make this drink. I'm including it here so that you can use it in a desperate situation that involves access to ketchup, shitty beer, and little else—if you find yourself in a frat house or at a minor-league baseball game, for example. Or perhaps more likely in a crappy restaurant with bad drinks and terrible beer. Dropping a few packets of ketchup and some dashes of hot sauce can do wonders for a sub-bar brew.

Makes 1 drink

12 to 16 ounces **bland lager beer**

2 **ketchup packets** (1 ounce / 2 tablespoons)

3 or 4 dashes **Cholula or other hot sauce** (optional)

Pinch of **salt**

Pinch of **freshly ground black pepper***

Optional Garnish Lime wedge

In a glass, combine the drink ingredients and stir to mix. Garnish with a lime wedge, if available.

NOTE You can also mix this directly in the beer can, but be sure that your first few swigs swing the can enough to slosh the beer around with the other ingredients.

---

* It's probably not freshly ground, let's be honest.

FEELING ADVENTUROUS

These drinks are meant to get you out of your comfort zone through unexpected combinations or with structures that break with conventional patterns. This chapter will serve as your guide to show you that there is life beyond established, tried-and-true frameworks. For anyone starting out learning a new skill, it's obviously imperative that you first learn the rules. That is, until you get to a certain point. True mastery of a skill comes from knowing the rules *and* how to break them when necessary.

The Stonewall Baby

I served this cocktail for my husband Michael's fortieth birthday party.[*] He was born on June 27, 1969, which is the night when activists like Marsha P. Johnson and Sylvia Rivera clashed with the police during a raid of the Stonewall Inn, the famous gay bar in New York City's Greenwich Village. This date is regarded as a watershed moment for the LGBTQIA civil rights movement, and so Michael often refers to himself as a "Stonewall baby." While the name of the drink tells the story of the historical significance of the date, the recipe does not. The ingredients are simply Michael's favorites. So no, the drink is not rainbow-colored, nor do any of the ingredients relate to the Stonewall Riots. It's simply a modified bourbon sour.

This drink is somewhat similar to the Preserves Sour (page 124), with the addition of ¼ ounce of simple syrup, which softens some of the acidity, as well as a dash of bitters, which provides aromatic complexity.

Makes 1 drink

2 ounces **bourbon, such as Maker's Mark**

¾ ounce **fresh lemon juice**

¼ ounce **Simple Syrup** (page 68)

1 tablespoon **blueberry preserves**

1 dash **Peychaud's bitters**

Garnish Lemon peel

In a shaker, combine the drink ingredients. Add ice and shake for 15 seconds. Strain into a chilled coupe. Garnish with a lemon peel, expressed and then perched on the rim.

---

[*] During the party, Michael got up to give a speech and at the end of it he proposed to me in front of all my friends, my coworkers, and my parents. It would have been mortifying if it hadn't been so adorable.

Alaska

This drink is a doozy—it's literally just 3 ounces of full-proof spirit. Don't be scared, though. It's a delicious doozy. I always come back to this under-the-radar forgotten classic when I want something strong but refreshing, something to sip on slowly. The bright herbal flavors of the gin and Chartreuse combine in a thunderous bolt of liquid lightning.

Makes 1 drink

2¼ ounces **gin**
¾ ounce **yellow Chartreuse**

In a mixing glass or shaking tin, combine the ingredients. Add ice and stir for 20 seconds. Strain into an ice-filled old fashioned glass.

Mill Valley Cooler

Watermelon is one of my favorite foods, and tequila is one of my favorite spirits, so naturally I put the two together as often as I can. Here, the spicy notes from the tequila are ramped up with the cinnamon infusion and supported by the Bénédictine.

If you're going to go to the trouble of juicing watermelon, save this recipe for a summer party where you'll be serving a few rounds of the coolers. You can even multiply the recipe by 10 and do it as a pitcher or a punch.

Makes 1 drink

1½ ounces **Cinnamon Tequila** (recipe follows)

¾ ounce **fresh watermelon juice**

½ ounce **Bénédictine**

¼ ounce **fresh lime juice**

Garnish Orange peel

In a shaker, combine the drink ingredients. Add ice and shake for 15 seconds. Strain into an ice-filled Collins glass. Express the orange peel over the top, then discard the peel before serving.

CINNAMON TEQUILA
Makes 1 (750mL) bottle

1 (750mL) bottle of **blanco tequila** (see Note)

2 small **cinnamon sticks**

In a medium-size container, combine the tequila and cinnamon sticks. Let it sit, covered, at room temperature for at least 10 hours.

Strain the tequila through a gold coffee filter, discarding the solids, and pour the tequila back into the original bottle. Store at room temperature for up to 1 year.

NOTE I like to infuse a full bottle of this because it's delicious and can be used in a variety of drinks, but feel free to halve this recipe.

Flower Powers

Green pepper and kumquats is not the most obvious combination, but the pairing of these two fruits* creates a deliciously intriguing combination of bright herbal flavors that are balanced by the mellow amber tones of Irish whiskey. It's a tight, compact drink with tons of acidity and complexity.

Makes 1 drink

2 **kumquats**

1 (1-inch) piece **green bell pepper, seeded**

1¾ ounces **Irish whiskey** (see Note)

¼ ounce **St-Germain**

¼ ounce **Honey Syrup** (page 186)

⅛ ounce **fresh lemon juice**

Optional Garnish Edible orchid

In a shaker, muddle the kumquats and green pepper together until crushed. Add the whiskey, St-Germain, honey syrup, and lemon juice. Add ice and shake for 15 seconds. Fine-strain into a chilled coupe. Garnish with an edible orchid, if you like.

NOTE I like to use Powers whiskey here, mostly because it helps the drink's name make sense—and it's a nice alternative to Jameson if you're looking to broaden your Irish whiskey repertoire—but it's not completely necessary.

---

* Green pepper is a fruit! I know, mind-blowing.

Picky Picky

My friend and former colleague, the all-around amazing Jordan Salcito, is the creator of Ramona,* a canned wine cooler made with sparkling white wine and grapefruit juice. When Jordan asked me to create a cocktail with it for Ramona's social media channels, I was thrilled for the opportunity to do something really unexpected.

Conventionally, you'd keep the drink refreshing and light to go along with the fruity vibe of Ramona. But I put this drink together with Scotch and bitters to showcase it in a different light. Taking flavors out of their usual context—in this case, pairing grapefruit with Scotch instead of the more expected gin or tequila—is a great way to make drinks more interesting . . . and more delicious.

Makes 1 drink

1½ ounces **un-peated blended Scotch**

½ ounce **St-Germain**

½ ounce **blue curaçao, such as Senior Curaçao**

4 dashes **orange bitters**

4 ounces / ½ cup **Ramona grapefruit wine cooler**

In a mixing glass or shaking tin, combine the Scotch, St-Germain, curaçao, and bitters. Add ice and stir for 20 seconds. Strain into a chilled white wine glass. Top with the Ramona.

---

* The Picky Picky is named after the cat who belonged to Beverly Cleary's iconic character Ramona Quimby.

Lion's Tooth

Roasted dandelion-root tea is a great placeholder for coffee for someone like me, who, due to a lifelong chronic anxiety disorder, can have only so much caffeine before spiraling out. I thought it would be fun to incorporate this ingredient into a cocktail because it has a deep, complex roasted flavor with a very accessible amount of bitterness. Structurally, this drink resembles a Manhattan, with the sherry and herbal liqueurs standing in for the vermouth, providing acidity and aromatics.

Makes 1 drink

2 ounces **Roasted Dandelion Root-Infused Rye** (recipe follows)

¾ ounce **Palo Cortado sherry**

½ ounce **yellow Chartreuse**

¼ ounce **St-Germain**

In a mixing glass or shaking tin, combine the drink ingredients. Add ice and stir for 20 seconds. Strain into a chilled coupe.

ROASTED DANDELION ROOT-INFUSED RYE
Makes about 10 ounces / 1¼ cups

12 ounces / 1½ cups **rye**

6 **roasted dandelion-root tea bags**

In a medium container, combine the rye and the tea bags. Steep for 10 minutes, until the spirit is infused. Remove the tea bags, being sure to squeeze out as much liquid as possible before discarding them. Store in a glass container at room temperature for up to 1 year.

Oki-Nomi
(オキ飲み)

This drink is a hot mess, but like many hot messes,* it's deliciously fun. It has a lot going on and it's about to go off the rails, but it somehow manages to keep it together.

The kind of rum you use isn't super important in this drink, just as long as it's dark. You should, however, make the effort to find Okinawan Awamori shochu. It's a rich and smoky spirit that complements the passion fruit and the crème de cacao. Okonomiyaki sauce is an unholy yet delicious blend of tomato paste, vinegar, carrots, prunes, apricots, and dried sardines; it provides a ready-made hit of complexity, including a bit of savory funk from the tiny fishies.

The name here takes a bit of explanation, but bear with me—it's worth it. The drink is inspired by Okinawa, the tropical Japanese island, hence the "oki." But it also contains okonomiyaki sauce, and nomi is a form of the Japanese verb "to drink." You kind of have to know Japanese to really appreciate this, but I hope even if you don't, I have demonstrated to you that I am a very smart and clever person indeed.

Makes 1 drink

1 ounce **aged rum**

1 ounce **Awamori shochu**

¾ ounce **fresh lime juice**

¼ ounce **white crème de cacao**

¼ ounce **passion fruit purée, such as Boiron**

¼ ounce **okonomiyaki sauce**

¼ ounce **cane syrup**

Garnishes Lime wheel, cocktail umbrella, and passion fruit half (optional)

In a shaker, combine the drink ingredients. Add ice and shake for 15 seconds. Strain the drink into an ice-filled tiki mug. Garnish with a lime wheel and an umbrella, and a fresh passion fruit half, if you have one.

---

* me

Soy Sauce Old Fashioned

When I was at Momofuku, I created a drink based around Bonji, a proprietary ingredient made for the restaurants. Bonji is like soy sauce, which is the pressed juice of soybeans fermented using a special koji (mold strain). At Momofuku, rye grains are used instead of soybeans, creating an earthy and slightly spicy alternative. I combined the Bonji with black sugar from Okinawa to serve as the sweetener in a simple bourbon Old Fashioned that's intriguing and unique while still being accessible to a broad audience. Since Bonji isn't commercially available, I've substituted regular soy sauce in this adaptation. I'd recommend springing for some nice, high-quality soy sauce from a specialty store. Here we're using soy sauce as the liquid in a sugar syrup made with black sugar, which offers a rich, sweet contrast to the salty soy sauce and picks up on the spicy, woody notes in the bourbon.

Makes 1 drink

2 ounces **bourbon**

¼ ounce **Black Sugar Syrup** (recipe follows)

2 dashes **Angostura bitters**

1 dash **orange bitters**

Garnish Orange peel

In a mixing glass or shaking tin, combine the drink ingredients. Add ice and stir for 15 seconds. Strain the drink into a rocks glass filled with ice. Garnish with an orange peel on the rim.

BLACK SUGAR SYRUP
Makes about 1 cup

100g **black sugar**

3½ ounces **filtered water**

1 ounce **high-quality soy sauce**

In a blender, combine the ingredients and let them soak for 5 to 10 minutes, until the sugar has softened. Blend on high speed for 3 minutes, until the sugar has been incorporated. Let the mixture settle for a few minutes before using (it will be frothy). Store in an airtight container in the refrigerator for up to 2 weeks or in the freezer for up to 6 months.

The Summer Quartet

I refer to shaken citrus drinks with four equal parts, like the Last Word (page 99), as Quartets, and this is a classic example of one. It has four ingredients that play off each other's intensity and distinctiveness. Often, not-great cocktails will try to clumsily incorporate lots of strongly flavored ingredients, and the result is muddied and neither objectively nor subjectively delicious. The key with Quartets is the limitation of three ingredients (plus citrus), so you have to be thoughtful when selecting those ingredients, finding the right balance of harmony and assertiveness.

Makes 1 drink

¾ ounce **sotol** (see Note)

¾ ounce **St. George raspberry liqueur**

¾ ounce **Amaro Montenegro**

¾ ounce **fresh lime juice**

Pinch of **salt**

In a shaker, combine the drink ingredients. Add ice and shake for 15 seconds. Strain into a chilled coupe.

NOTE Sotol is a spirit that comes from northern Mexico, where it is made from the desert spoon plant. It's intense and earthy. It may not be accessible in your area. You can substitute mezcal and the drink will still work fine.

BALANCE EXERCISES

The purpose of these exercises is to help you to develop your own understanding of objective and subjective deliciousness. In them you will make three variations on the two most primal of cocktails: the daiquiri and the Old Fashioned. One version will follow the standard measure of balance, and two will be off in some way. I'll explain which version is generally accepted to be the most objectively delicious—balanced—and which two aren't, and why. While some of the versions might not be totally "wrong," by pulling the levers on some common balance points, it should help you understand your preferences better. If you want the full experience, don't peek ahead to see which is which before tasting and judging for yourself.

Daiquiri, Three Ways*

Although this is a simple three-ingredient drink, it demonstrates the knobs you can adjust to vary the balance of virtually every drink that's shaken with citrus.

Daiquiri A

1½ ounces **white rum**

¾ ounce **fresh lime juice**

¾ ounce **Simple Syrup**
  (page 68)

In a shaker, combine the drink ingredients. Fill with ice and shake vigorously for 15 seconds. Strain into a chilled cocktail glass.

Daiquiri B

2 ounces **white rum**

¾ ounce **fresh lime juice**

¾ ounce **Simple Syrup**
  (page 68)

In a shaker, combine the drink ingredients. Fill with ice and shake vigorously for 15 seconds. Strain into a chilled cocktail glass.

Daiquiri C

2 ounces **white rum**

½ ounce **fresh lime juice**

1 ounce **Simple Syrup**
  (page 68)

In a shaker, combine the drink ingredients. Fill with ice and shake vigorously for 15 seconds. Strain into a chilled cocktail glass.

---

* If this isn't the name of a tropical-themed gay porn, it should be. Sean Cody, hit me up.

Take a sip of all three and ask yourself these questions for each version:

1. How perceptible are the individual ingredients?

2. How balanced is it in terms of acid, sweetness, and alcohol? Does it taste watery? Too strong?

3. Which is your favorite?

Let these three drinks sit out at room temperature for five minutes, taste them each again, and ask yourself the same three questions.

Wait ten more minutes and taste them again. Note how the drinks change as they warm—the ingredients start to settle and air bubbles dissipate.

Is it better this way, or did you prefer them cold and fresh?

The version that I consider to be the best is Daiquiri B right after it's poured from the shaker, because it has the best balance among the three ingredients and dilution and still has the aeration from shaking. But do you agree? (Is there a fourth variation that you might like even better?)

Old Fashioned, Three Ways*

Here is another low-ingredient-count drink that can reveal where the balance points lie in stirred cocktails.

Old Fashioned A

2 ounces **rye**

¼ ounce **Demerara Syrup**
  (page 72)

2 dashes **Angostura bitters**

1 dash **orange bitters**

In a mixing glass or shaking tin, combine the drink ingredients. Fill with ice and stir for 20 seconds. Strain into an ice-filled old fashioned glass.

Old Fashioned B

1½ ounces **rye**

½ ounce **Demerara Syrup**
  (page 72)

2 dashes **Angostura bitters**

1 dash **orange bitters**

In a mixing glass or shaking tin, combine the drink ingredients. Fill with ice and stir for 20 seconds. Strain into an ice-filled old fashioned glass.

Old Fashioned C

2 ounces **rye**

¼ ounce **Demerara Syrup**
  (page 72)

In a mixing glass or shaking tin, combine the drink ingredients. Fill with ice and stir for 20 seconds. Strain into an ice-filled old fashioned glass.

---

* I'm also making a retro-themed porn.

Take a sip of all three and ask yourself these questions for each version:

1. How perceptible are the individual ingredients?

2. How balanced is it in terms of sweetness, bitterness, and alcohol? Does it taste watery? Too strong?

3. Which is your favorite?

Let these three drinks sit out at room temperature for five minutes, taste them each again, and ask yourself the same three questions.

Wait ten more minutes and taste them again. Note how the drinks change as they warm—the ice is diluting the drink as it melts.

Are they better after sitting out for a while, or did you prefer them fresh?

My guess is that of the three, you prefer Old Fashioned A, which is generally regarded as the standard recipe. Maybe you even liked it a bit more after it had been sitting for a few minutes. Which one was your favorite? Don't be afraid to have a different choice now that you've explored your preferences—that's what this exercise is all about.

FURTHER READING

Cocktail Books

DAVE ARNOLD
Liquid Intelligence: The Art and Science of the Perfect Cocktail

I had the pleasure of working alongside Dave while he was at Booker and Dax, a bar that was operated by Momofuku, for five years. His vision is that of uncompromising precision informed by a deep technical knowledge of food science. There's a lot in his book that most people won't be able to accomplish, but it's worth the read—getting inside Dave's head, even slightly, will lend tremendous benefits to your drink-making practice. And it's just an overall enjoyable and informative book.

HARRY CRADDOCK
The Savoy Cocktail Book

A super stylish book filled with hundreds of recipes, this is a great one to page through when you're looking for ideas. Not all the drinks are delicious, and plenty of the products Craddock calls for are discontinued or reformulated. But the sheer number of cocktails in this book makes it an essential source of inspiration for professional and amateur bartenders alike.

JIM MEEHAN
The PDT Cocktail Book: The Complete Bartender's Guide from the Celebrated Speakeasy

I really don't have enough good things to say about this book, which is easy enough for amateurs and deep enough for professionals. It's accessible and comprehensive, and it instructs the reader in a wide variety of cocktail styles and techniques. Plus, a few of my recipes are in it, which is a huge ego boost.

JIM MEEHAN
Meehan's Bartender Manual

A follow-up to *The PDT Cocktail Book*, this one is encyclopedic and professional-focused. Consider tackling this epic tome as the equivalent of getting your MA in bartending. Dense, fact-filled, and delicious.

JEFFREY MORGENTHALER
The Bar Book: Elements of Cocktail Technique

In one of the most accessible technical bar books, Jeff takes a scientific approach to the hows and whys of making drinks without getting too esoteric or self-serious.

SASHA PETRASKE
Regarding Cocktails

Published posthumously, this book is the best way to get a feel for who this man was. Sasha was one of the founding figures of the modern cocktail renaissance, and his influence can be felt everywhere. Even though I never worked for him or at any of the many bars he helped open, his way of thinking about cocktails has informed mine to a great degree.

GARY REGAN
The Joy of Mixology: The Consummate Guide to the Bartender's Craft

This was the first cocktail book I ever read, and it was a fabulous foundation to build on. There is a recently revised and updated edition—this book's original publication predated the modern cocktail renaissance by a few years—and it's a fantastic way to get into the mind-set of a bartender. Even if you never set foot behind a real bar, the lessons in this book will make you better at making drinks.

Drinks Books

DAVID BROOM
The World Atlas of Whisky

I picked up this book at a secondhand bookstore in Harrisburg, Pennsylvania, and it blew my mind. It focuses largely on Scotch but still covers all the major (and minor) whiskey-making regions of the world. It showed me that the spirits world is as rich and varied as that of wine.

IAIN GATELY
Drink: A Cultural History of Alcohol

It should be pretty self-evident from the title what this book is about, but I cannot overstate the significance of the work Iain has done toward deepening our understanding of the forces that have shaped our world. Think of this as the alcohol rendition of Mark Kurlansky's *Salt* (also excellent).

BRAD THOMAS PARSONS
Amaro: The Spirited World of Bittersweet, Herbal Liqueurs, with Cocktails, Recipes, and Formulas

While vanity and narcissism are definitely reasons why I'm recommending books that I appear in, this book would be in here even if it did not contain a handful of full-page and full-color photos of me. Amaro is a mysterious and understudied class of liqueurs, and Brad's book does an excellent job of introducing us to this wonderful category.

AMY STEWART
The Drunken Botanist: The Plants That Create the World's Best Drinks

Astonishingly well researched, this book is a must for anyone really looking to get to know the plants that help us make delicious drinks. It's extremely inspiring when I'm looking for botanicals to use creatively, and it's also full of fascinating cocktail-party trivia.

DAVID WONDRICH
Imbibe! From Absinthe Cocktail to Whiskey Smash, a Salute in Stories and Drinks to "Professor" Jerry Thomas, Pioneer of the American Bar

A deeply enjoyable trip back to a time that many might consider the golden age of cocktails—the 1860s—and an introduction to one of the first celebrity bartenders, Jerry Thomas. It helped me in my early career to understand that no one is ever just a bartender, and that the job can be a stepping-stone to fame and (modest) fortune.

Science Books

BRIAN HOEFLING
Distilled Knowledge: The Science Behind Drinking's Greatest Myths, Legends, and Unanswered Questions

Brian takes a *MythBusters* approach to some of the lore and misconceptions about alcohol and its effects on the body. Super informative and, while technical, accessible to most readers.

HAROLD McGEE
On Food and Cooking: The Science and Lore of the Kitchen

Reading this book is a commitment, but I highly recommend that anyone with even a passing interest in food and beverage go through it at least once. It really helps you understand why certain techniques are used in cooking, and it will also help you to become vastly more self-sufficient in both the kitchen and the bar.

MARK SCHATZKER
The Dorito Effect: The Surprising New Truth About Food and Flavor

This book is as important as it is informative, with some really cool anecdotes along the way. It gives the reader an extremely well-reported look into the current state of our understanding of the complex interactions among our bodies, our minds, food, nutrition, culture, and public policy.

GORDON SHEPHERD
Neurogastronomy: How the Brain Creates Flavor and Why It Matters

I have a huge interest in how the mind and body work to deliver the sensation of flavor to our conscious awareness, and this book is what sparked it. It is heavy on the science and at times over even my head, but if you power through, and are okay with not understanding absolutely everything, you won't regret reading it.

Acknowledgments and Thanks

My agent, Nicole Tourtelot (Princess Carolyn), because this book literally would not have happened without her.

The team at Clarkson Potter, particularly Amanda Englander, who made this book so much more (a.k.a. better) than I ever thought it could be. As well as Allison Renzulli, David Hawk, Ian Dingman, Jessica Heim, Stephanie Huntwork, and Terry Deal.

The brilliant and talented Sarah Tanat-Jones, for her exquisite illustrations.

Jim Meehan, for the years of mentorship and the immensely flattering foreword to this book.

My family and friends (a.k.a. nonbiological family), for their love and support: Victoria deBary, Ned deBary, Paul deBary, Katrina Chapman, Cynthia Sleight, Brett and Victor Nee, Jonathan Rousell (Weeza), Leslie and Charles Rousell (also Weeza), Joan and George Hellman, Kerrin Egalka, Jena Derman, Karen Fu (Baby Smooshface), Anna-Lisa Campos, Alex Pemoulié, Amanda Dolan, Elizabeth Haynes and Mahender Nathan, Hugo Goodwin, Daniel de la Nuez, Leland Benton, Olivia Henry, and Sarah Todd.

My industry colleagues (whom I also consider friends and family) who have in some way left an indelible mark: Alison Roman, Amber Duarte, Anne Robinson, Ariane Hardjowirogo, Arielle Johnson, Beth Lieberman, Brad Thomas Parsons, Brette Warshaw, Charles Vexenat, Christina Tosi, Christina Turley, Daniel Eun, Dave Arnold, Dave Chang, Dave Wondrich, Don Lee, Drew Salmon, Elizabeth Tilton, Eunjean Song, Greg Bohem, Hillary Dixler, Jack Schramm, Jake Lewis, Jane Danger, Jeff Bell, JJ Pyle, John Deragon, Jordan Salcito, Julia Bainbridge, Kate Krader, Kevin Diedrich, Lurie De La Rosa, Matt Rudofker, Nate Dumas, Nick Bennet, Pamela Wiznitzer, Paul Carmichael, Peter Meehan, Rachel Piazza, Rebecca Palkovics, Sam Penix, Sara Jimenez-Curtola, Sean Gray, Sean Hoard (Sharky), Su Wong Ruiz, Susan Choung, Tara Macmullen, Theresa Paopao, Tim Maslow, Tony Kim, and Victor Lopez.

And my best Smoop, Michael Remaley.

Index

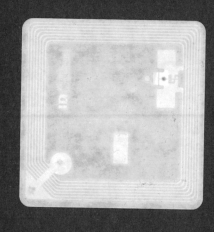